ELEANOR ROOSEVELT

Her Life in Pictures

ELEANOR ROOSEVELT

By Richard Harrity

and Ralph G. Martin

Her Life in Pictures

DUELL, SLOAN AND PEARCE
NEW YORK

Library of Congress Catalogue Card Number: 58–12266

First edition

Manufactured in the United States of America

CREDITS:

Bachrach, 185
Bette E. Barber, 66 (top)
The Bettmann Archive, 38 (bottom)
Brown Brothers, 49
Burck, Augusta (Georgia) *Chronicle*, 182
The Byron Collection, Museum of the City of New York, 25
Nancy Cook, 98, 99, 107 (bottom), 145 (bottom)
Culver Service, 33 (top), 65, 218 (top), 242, 253 (top)
Franklin D. Roosevelt Library, 9, 23, 24, 26, 27, 29, 30, 31 (top left and bottom), 32, 33 (bottom), 34, 35, 36, 37, 38 (top), 39, 40, 41, 42, 43, 44, 47, 50, 51, 52, 53, 66 (bottom), 67, 68, 69, 70, 74 (top), 75 (bottom), 76, 77, 79, 80, 84, 85, 86, 97, 104 (top), 107 (top), 110, 133, 134 (bottom), 136 (top), 159 (top), 175, 177, 178, 179, 180, 181, 190, 193 (bottom), 199 (bottom), 204, 213, 214, 220 (top), 226, 228, 229 (top), 231 (bottom), 232, 233, 234, 235
Free Lance Photographers Guild, Inc., 62, 73, 78, 83, 95 (top), 100 (top), 112 (bottom), 128, 129, 139, 150, 172 (top), 184, 216, 218 (bottom)
Dr. A. David Gurewitsch, 244 (bottom), 247
Harris & Ewing, 149
International News Photo, 28, 45, 46, 63, 71, 72, 74 (bottom), 81 (bottom), 87, 95 (bottom), 106 (top), 109, 112 (top), 126, 143, 146 (bottom), 154 (bottom), 156, 170, 171, 183, 188, 189, 200 (top), 219, 227, 248 (top)
Knickerbocker News (Albany, New York), 101, 103, 108 (top)
Jackie Martin, 174
New York Daily News Photo, 114, 134 (top), 137 (bottom), 154 (top), 173 (top)
New York Public Library, 132
Press Information Bureau, Government of India, 229 (bottom)
Sammy Schulman (International News Photo), 249
Marten Tafel, 252–53
Julius Tannenbaum, 236, 237
UN Photo, 215, 217 (bottom)
Underwood & Underwood of Washington, D.C., 127
UPI, 75 (top), 81 (top), 82, 96, 106 (bottom), 108 (bottom), 111, 113 (top), 135 (top), 138 (top), 141 (bottom), 142, 145 (top), 147, 155, 158 (top), 159 (bottom), 176, 186 (top), 200 (bottom), 202, 203, 217 (top), 222 (bottom), 223 (bottom), 224, 231 (top), 238 (bottom), 239, 244 (top), 245
U.S. Air Transport Command, 194 (bottom), 195 (bottom)
U.S. Army Photo, 195 (top)
U.S. Army Signal Corps Photo, 194 (top)
U.S. Park Service, 64
Arnold L. Weissberger, 246
Wide World Photos, 8, 25, 100 (bottom), 104 (bottom), 105, 113 (bottom), 115, 116, 117, 130, 131, 135 (bottom), 136 (bottom), 137 (top), 138 (bottom), 140, 144, 146 (top), 148, 153, 157, 158 (bottom), 172 (bottom), 173 (bottom), 186 (bottom), 187, 192 (top), 197, 198, 199 (top), 201, 220 (bottom), 221, 222 (top), 223 (top), 225, 230, 238 (top), 240, 241, 243, 248 (bottom), 250, 251, 254

Thomas Y. Crowell Company for permission to quote from *Eleanor Roosevelt* by Sally Knapp.
Harper & Brothers for permission to quote from *This Is My Story* by Eleanor Roosevelt.
Look magazine for permission to quote from articles by Eleanor Roosevelt.
New York Times Sunday Magazine for permission to quote from an interview with Mrs. Roosevelt.
Charles Scribner's Sons for permission to quote from *Hunting Big Game in the Eighties* edited by Eleanor Roosevelt.

Contents

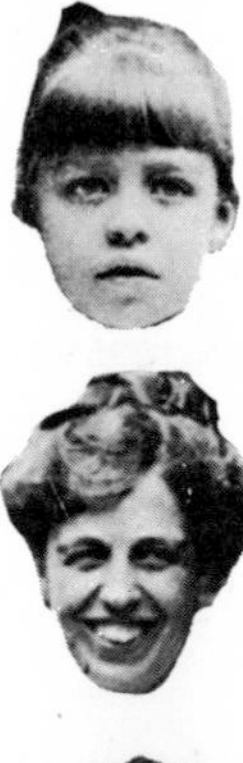

Acknowledgments

This is to acknowledge gratefully the help given us by Herman Kahn, director of the Franklin D. Roosevelt Library at Hyde Park, New York, and the members of his staff: Margaret L. Suckley, William J. Nichols, Robert L. Jacoby, Raymond H. Corry, William F. Stickle, Jerome V. Deyo, Louise H. Evans.

Our thanks also to Mary S. Lindsey and Mason Tolman of the New York State Library.

And for their important cooperation, our added appreciation to Herblock, Dr. A. David Gurewitsch, Victor Hammer, Joseph Rotwein, Dick Hanley, Ed Plaut, and Shirley Green.

Finally, our particular thanks to Nancy Cook, Marion Dickerman, and the Dowager Marchioness of Reading.

For

Ailie and Marge

CHANDOR
NEW YORK
by the painter

Eleanor Roosevelt wrote this entry in a diary in 1899 when she was fifteen years old:

"Nov. 13 To be the thing we seem
To do the thing we deem
enjoined by duty
To walk in faith nor dream
Of questioning God's scheme
of truth & beauty.

It is very hard to do what this verse says, so hard I never succeed & I am always questioning & questioning because I cannot understand & never succeed in doing what I mean to do, never, never. I suppose I don't really try. I can feel it in me sometimes that I can do much more than I am doing & I mean to try till *I do* succeed."

1. The Early Years

Anna Eleanor Roosevelt's mother and father—Anna Hall, a descendant of Robert Livingston, one of the signers of the Declaration of Independence, and Elliott Roosevelt, eighth in a direct line from Claes Martenszan van Rosenvelt, who emigrated from Holland in the seventeenth century and founded the Roosevelt family in America—were charter members of the exclusive New York social world which was then limited to the Four Hundred and took itself very seriously.

Anna Hall Roosevelt was a reigning beauty of that select society composed of well-bred ladies and gentlemen, who lived graciously, in substantial homes, observed rigid rules of decorum and behavior, and did their duty to their neighbors, which included polite philanthropy or, as it was then called, "kindness to the poor." Elliott Roosevelt, born into that same world, had a wider range of activity and experience and a deeper interest in people. Before his marriage he had traveled around the world; lived at a frontier post in Texas; and hunted big game with his older brother Theodore, later President of the United States. He also had a better understanding of the poor and the afflicted through the work he did in behalf of the crippled children in the New York Orthopaedic Hospital, which was founded by his father. "He loved people for the fineness that was in them and his friends might be newsboys or millionaires," was the way his daughter once described him. "Their occupations, their possessions, meant nothing to him, only they themselves counted."

When Anna Eleanor Roosevelt, the first child of this union, was born on October 11, 1884, her father hailed her arrival as "a miracle from heaven." As she grew into a solemn-faced and plain-looking child, however, her mother could not conceal her disappointment that her daughter had not inherited the Hall beauty.

"I can remember," Mrs. Eleanor Roosevelt wrote in *This Is My Story*, "standing in the door, very often with my finger in my mouth—which was, of course, forbidden—and I can see the look in her eyes and hear the tone of her voice as she said: 'Come in, Granny.' If a visitor was there, she might turn and say: 'She is such a funny child, so old-fashioned, that we always call her Granny.' I wanted to sink through the floor in shame and I felt I was apart from the boys [her younger brothers, Elliott and Hall]."

Her father always called her "Little Nell" after the gentle character in Charles Dickens's *The Old Curiosity Shop* and made her his constant companion, taking her with him when he visited the Orthopaedic Hospital, teaching her to ride, reading poetry to her, and telling her about his travels. There was a deep bond between the two, and when, without giving her any explanation, Elliott Roosevelt suddenly disappeared from their home, the six-year-old child was broken-hearted.

She and her two brothers were then living with their mother

in the New York City home of their grandmother, Mrs. Valentine Hall. For weeks after her father left, Eleanor, desperately missing his companionship and affection, kept a day-long vigil at the front windows of the house hoping for a sight of him in the street outside. When he did not return, she retreated into herself and created a dream world in which her father, gay and charming, was always with her. Once when her mother and her two young aunts, Maude and Edith Hall, thought she was asleep, she overheard them discussing her father's "weakness," but it was not until years later that she learned that it was simply a polite term for alcoholism.

Finally, he wrote his "Dearest little Nell" a letter that held a promise of her dream world coming true. "Because Father is not with you is not because he doesn't love you for I love you tenderly and dearly—and maybe soon I'll come back well and strong and we will have such good times together as we used to have."

"My Sweet little Nell:

Thank you my little daughter for writing me so precious a little 'love token.' I miss you terribly and think of you and the loved little brothers all the time."

Once she saw her father for a brief moment on Fifth Avenue and when she returned to her Grandmother Hall's home she immediately wrote him a letter, to which he replied:

"My Darling Little Nell:

I have received your beautifully written French note of the 26th; thank you my darling for writing to me. Since that sweet sight of you on the Avenue I have been traveling about the country and also quite ill."

In December 1892, Anna Hall Roosevelt contracted diphtheria and died, naming her mother the guardian of the three children. Death was as deep a mystery to eight-year-old Eleanor as was the continued absence of her father, except that it was the agency which was finally bringing him back to her.

On his return from southwest Virginia, where he had been exiled, Elliott Roosevelt, a sick man, who was drinking himself to death, was confronted with a double tragedy. The wife whom he adored had died before he could even begin to make up the hurt he had caused her, and his mother-in-law told him that he could not be trusted to take care of his own children. Yet he talked to his little daughter with enthusiasm about the future, the trips they would take together, the places they would see, and most important of all, the home of their own which they would one day share. But the tender, loving, and lonely child was destined not to have that home.

The father went back to Virginia and sent her a letter containing this advice: "The next time you go walking get your maid to take you where they are building a house and watch the workmen bring one stone after another and place it on top of the one gone before or alongside then think there are a lot of funny little workmen running about in your small golden head called 'ideas' which are carrying a lot of stones like small bodies called 'Facts' and these 'Ideas' are being directed by your teachers in various ways by 'Persuasion,' 'Instruction,' 'Love,' 'Truth' to place all these 'Fact Stones' on top of and alongside each other in your dear Golden Head until they build a beautiful house called 'Education.' "

She made a promise to work and study hard and wrote to him faithfully, but months went by without any letters from him. Then sometime before her tenth birthday she received a letter.

"Darling Little Nell:

What must you think of your father who has not written in so long? I have after all been very busy, quite ill, at intervals not able to move from my bed for days. . . .

"How is your pony and the dogs at Tivoli, too. . . ?
. . . with tender affection
ever devotedly,
your Father,
Elliott Roosevelt."

"There were no more letters after this for me or anyone else," Mrs. Roosevelt recalled in 1951, "for he died in the summer of 1894 and with him went all the realities of companionship which he had suggested for the future but . . . he lived in my dreams to this day and still does."

The newspaper in Abingdon, Virginia, ran this editorial comment on Elliott Roosevelt when he died:

> This gentleman has been a member of this community for the past two years and although his stay was so brief, it was long enough for him to make the impress as a whole souled, genial gentleman, courteous and kind at all times, with an ever ready cheer for the enterprising or help to the weak. His name was a byword among the needy, and his charities were always as abundant as they were unostentatious.

With her father's death, a new life began for Eleanor and her brother Hall—Elliott, the third child, had died a few months after his mother. Grandmother Hall was now their guardian. The Hall family treated the two orphans with great kindness and always made them feel at home, whether in their town house in New York or on their estate at Tivoli, up the Hudson. Grandmother Hall was a stern disciplinarian to whom DUTY was a sacred word and Eleanor Roosevelt was made to follow a strict regime, with emphasis on religious training.

"Sunday was, indeed, a day set apart from other days, and some of the things decreed by my grandmother, who brought me up, I personally very much resented," Mrs. Roosevelt wrote

forty years later. "I could not play games on Sunday; I had to sit on the uncomfortable small seat in my grandmother's large Victoria and drive five miles to and from church; I had special books which I was only allowed to read on Sundays, and could not read the story in which I happened to be interested. But I really enjoyed learning the Bible verses and hymns, which always had to be memorized (in French) for Sunday morning, and I have never to this day quite got over the real pleasure of singing hymns on Sunday evening, after supper, as a family. These were agreeable things, and besides, your elders had more time to talk to you. They even took little people for very pleasant walks on Sunday afternoons, and in the winter I can remember open fires and books read aloud, which to this day carry me back to a happy atmosphere. But this religious training was not just an affair of Sundays—there were family prayers every morning, and you grew up with the feeling that you had a share in some great spiritual existence beyond the everyday round of happenings."

During the week, regular hours were devoted each day to practicing the piano, the study of languages, lessons in ballet, regular dancing classes with the children of her own world, instruction by carefully selected governesses in sewing, embroidery, the hemming of innumerable dish towels, darning. Nothing slipshod was ever tolerated. If she made a mistake in darning a stocking, a pair of scissors would snip it off, leaving a large hole for her to fill.

And on Sundays there were "good works," such as teaching Sunday school to the coachman's little daughter.

As a part of her training she was made to take part in the charitable work which was then deemed proper for young girls in her position. She accompanied her aunts when they went to sing at the Bowery Mission, and helped her uncle, Valentine G. Hall, decorate Christmas trees in Hell's Kitchen, one of the worst slum sections in New York City, learning at an early age how the underprivileged had to live. Once, when she was taken to the Orthopaedic Hospital, she stopped to chat with a crippled boy who was in a brace and, quickly sensing the other child's embarrassment, she showed him the steel brace she herself was wearing to correct a spinal curvature.

During the summer, when the Hall family moved to Oak Terrace, their country estate at Tivoli-on-the-Hudson near Poughkeepsie, her young aunts and uncles played games with her, but the only playmate of Eleanor Roosevelt's own age lived five miles away, and as a result she spent most of her free time with books and her dreams in a little house her grandmother had built for her in the woods. Her closest friend during this lonely period of her childhood at Tivoli was the hard-working farmer's wife, Mrs. Overhalse, who did the washing and ironing for the Hall family. She was a cheerful woman, and the child spent many happy hours chatting with her and helping her with the laundry. She was beginning to feel drawn to people "for the fineness that was in them."

When she was not putting in hours of study with private tutors, she helped take care of her young brother Hall and sought ways to be a useful member of the busy household. Duty was becoming a motivating force in her life, and in helping others she was finding her greatest satisfaction.

Once a year she went to visit her uncle, Theodore Roosevelt, on Long Island. She looked forward to those visits with a mixture of delight and dread. She loved to listen to her uncle Ted read poetry and stories to his children, but when the hero of San Juan Hill began to organize athletic games she again felt apart, since she was not proficient in sports and did not even know how to swim.

One year her uncle Ted gave a dance for the children and she was invited. Eleanor Roosevelt, who was tall at fourteen and rather ungainly, appeared in a party dress which, at the insistence of her grandmother, came above her knees, making her seem all legs. The other girls of her age wore skirts that came halfway down their legs, as was then the fashion. Painfully shy to begin with, this "different" dress increased her self-consciousness as she sat at the side of the dance floor. She had been sitting there for some time when her distant cousin, Franklin Roosevelt, walked across the floor and asked her to dance. They had first met when she was two years old and he was four and she rode on his back around the nursery at his mother's Hyde Park home. As they danced, her shyness disappeared and she talked with ease on many subjects. She had read every book she could lay her hands on in the library at Tivoli and had a lively appreciation of literature. The next day, in describing the dance to his mother, Franklin said: "Cousin Eleanor has a very good mind."

The real training of her mind began the following year when she was fifteen. Her grandmother Hall sent her to England to attend the Allenswood School near London. Mademoiselle Marie Souvestre, the headmistress, was a woman of character with a warm heart, and she took an immediate liking to her American pupil.

"She exerted perhaps the greatest influence on my girlhood," was the tribute paid to Mademoiselle Souvestre. "She liked Americans and attributed to them qualities of character and intelligence which shortly began to give me back some of the confidence that I had not felt since my father died."

Under Mademoiselle Souvestre's guidance she improved her French, mastered German and Italian, gained a good knowledge of history, and learned to be tolerant of the feelings and opinions of others, even though they were completely contrary to her own.

"As I look back," Mrs. Roosevelt recalled, "long years later I realized that Mademoiselle Souvestre was rather an extraordinary character. She often fought seemingly lost causes, but they were often won in the long run. The Dreyfus case was one of them. Captain Dreyfus was vindicated in the end, but for years before he was declared innocent, we who were under Mademoiselle Souvestre's influence heard every move in the case fought over and over again. I think I came to feel that the underdog was always the one to be championed.

"When the Boer War came along, Mademoiselle Souvestre was pro-Boer. She had a great many friends in government circles; in fact, one of her old pupils was a daughter of an Englishman high in the government at that time. But that did not deter her from being a pro-Boer running a girls' school in England or from her outspoken criticism of British policies. On the other hand, she was scrupulously fair and allowed the British girls to celebrate their victories in South Africa, although she would take the rest of us into her library and talk to us at length on the rights of small nations while the British celebration was going on.

"For three years I basked in her generous presence, and I think those three years did much to form my character and give me confidence to go through some of the trials that awaited me when I returned to the United States."

After finishing her studies at the Allenswood School, Eleanor Roosevelt returned to New York City, where she made her formal bow to society at an Assembly Ball in 1902. As a debutante she went to all the fashionable balls and parties and met many eligible young men, but her relatives wondered if she would ever attract any beaux.

Eleanor Roosevelt had other worries. During her school years in England, the Hall household had become a troubled one because of the heavy drinking of her two uncles, and she often had to search for them in the saloons along Sixth Avenue and bring them home. And since her grandmother had to worry about her own sons and was quite old, Eleanor Roosevelt also assumed responsibility of being a mother to her young brother Hall.

As service to others had become a part of her character and the word society had taken on a bigger meaning for her, Eleanor Roosevelt began to plan her life so that it combined social activity with social work. The young Eleanor taught calisthenics and dancing at the Rivington Street Settlement House and worked with the Consumers League investigating working conditions in sweatshops and garment factories.

She frequently saw her cousin, Franklin Roosevelt, who was then finishing his studies at Harvard. In 1903 he proposed to her. Eleanor Roosevelt was nineteen and he was twenty-one.

"I have only a few bright prospects now," he said.

"I have faith in you," she replied. "I'm sure you'll really amount to something someday."

Mrs. James Roosevelt was terribly upset about the engagement of her only son, a senior at college who planned to study law. Her son, however, had made up his mind, as he explained to her in a letter when he returned to Harvard:

> Dearest Mama:
>
> I know what pain I must have caused you and you know I wouldn't do it if I really could have helped it—*mais tu sais, me voilà*! That's all that could be said—I know my mind, have known

it for a long time, and know that I could never think otherwise. Result: I am the happiest man just now in the world; likewise the luckiest. And for you dear Mummy, you know that nothing can ever change what we have always been and always will be to each other—only now you have two children to love & to love you—and Eleanor as you know will always be a daughter to you in every true way.

Eleanor Roosevelt also wrote her future mother-in-law a letter:

8 East 76th Street (N.Y.)
Dec. 2, 1903
Wednesday

Dearest Cousin Sally,

I must write & thank you for being so kind to me yesterday. I know just how you feel & how hard it must be, but I do so want you to learn to love me a little. You must know that I will always try to do what you wish, for I have grown to love you very dearly during the past summer.

It is impossible for me to tell you how I feel toward Franklin, I can only say that my one great wish is always to prove worthy of him.

I am counting the days until the 12th when I hope Franklin & you will both be here again & if there is anything I can do for you you will write me, won't you?

With much love, dear Cousin Sally,

Always devotedly
Eleanor.

Mrs. James Roosevelt, a strong-willed and dominating woman, still felt that they were too young to announce their engagement and insisted that they wait for a year. She then took her son out of Harvard and made him go with her on a cruise to the West Indies, hoping that he would change his mind. Eleanor Roosevelt resented this, but when Franklin returned, their feelings had not changed and their engagement was finally announced.

In order to be near his fiancée Franklin Roosevelt entered Columbia instead of Harvard Law School, where he had originally planned to go.

Eleanor's Uncle Ted was elected to the presidency in 1904 and one newspaper editorial stated, "The United States was never nearer a social revolution than at the time Roosevelt became president." The new president invited the young engaged couple to attend his inauguration and, sitting on the platform behind him as he made his inaugural speech, they heard him make a statement—founded on faith in the American people which Franklin D. Roosevelt would put into practice twenty-eight years later—"All I ask is a square deal for every man."

Their marriage took place in the twin homes of Mrs. Henry Parish and Mrs. E. Livingston Ludlow, her relatives, at 6 and 8 East Seventy-sixth Street, New York City, on March 17, 1905, and President Roosevelt gave his niece away. Marchers in the St. Patrick's Day parade outside were singing "The Wearing of the Green," and the bride and groom had difficulty hearing each other's responses. When the ceremony was over, President Roosevelt congratulated them on keeping the Roosevelt name in the family, then proceeded to steal the show.

"Eleanor and Franklin often to this day," related Mrs. James Roosevelt, when her own son was president, "laugh over their chagrin when, immediately after the service had ended, and they took their places in the receiving line, they found that their guests were more concerned in greeting the President than in congratulating them. For an awful moment, the children insist, they were left entirely alone, while the crowd hovered around Mr. Roosevelt, shaking him by the hand."

At the end of his term at Columbia the following summer, the young married couple had their honeymoon in Europe. Both had made the grand tour with their families, both knew history, and both were as interested in people as they were in historic places, which made the trip a happy as well as an instructive one. While visiting friends in Scotland, however, Eleanor Roosevelt discovered with a shock that her knowledge of her own country was very meager. Her hostess asked her to explain the difference between our state and national governments and, despite the fact that her uncle had been a governor of a state and was then the president of the country, she was unable to give the answer. She promised herself that when she returned to America she would learn all she could about the government of her own country.

There was something else she would have to learn too—infinitely more difficult and more important to her—how to develop her own individuality while living with two strong and forceful personalities, her husband and her mother-in-law.

The christening dresses of Franklin D. Roosevelt (with locket) and Eleanor Roosevelt, who first met when she was two and he was four and she rode around on his back in the nursery of his Hyde Park home.

Eleanor Roosevelt's mother—Anna Hall Roosevelt, a descendant of Robert Livingston, one of the signers of the Declaration of Independence—was a reigning society beauty in the exclusive social world of the 1880's and the early '90's.

Her father, Elliott Roosevelt, standing beside his older brother, Theodore, later President of the United States, was eighth in a direct line from Claes Martenszan van Rosenvelt, a Hollander, who founded the Roosevelt family in America in the seventeenth century. Before his marriage, Elliott Roosevelt had traveled around the world, hunted big game, and lived at a frontier post in Texas.

Mr. and Mrs. Elliott Roosevelt were charter members of the Four Hundred, which took itself very seriously. It was a society composed of well-bred ladies and gentlemen who lived graciously in substantial homes, observed rigid rules of decorum and behavior, and did their duty to their neighbor including polite philanthropy or as it was then called, "kindness to the poor."

The country home of Eleanor Roosevelt's grandmother, Mrs. Valentine Hall, at Tivoli, New York, overlooking the Hudson River, built on land once part of the 163,000-acre estate of Robert Livingston. Eleanor Roosevelt spent her childhood there.

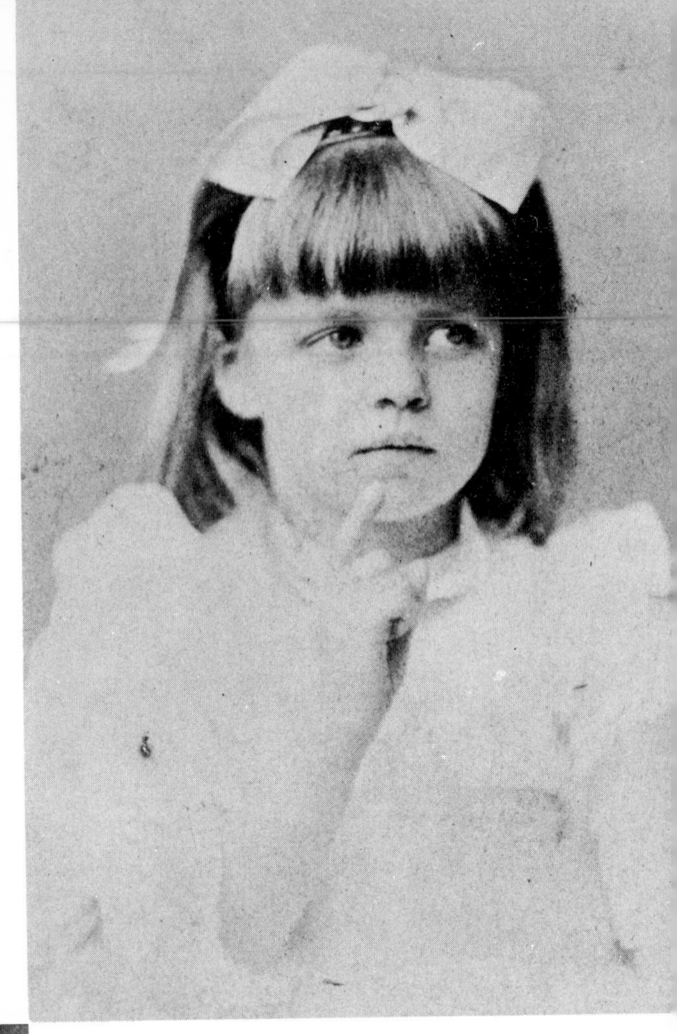

When Eleanor was born, her father hailed her arrival as "a miracle from heaven," and as she grew into a solemn-faced and plain-looking child, her mother, disappointed that she had not inherited the Hall beauty, called her "Granny."

Elliott Roosevelt named his daughter "Little Nell" after the gentle character in Charles Dickens's *The Old Curiosity Shop* and made her his constant companion, teaching her to ride, reading her stories, telling her about his travels, and taking her with him when he regularly visited the crippled children in the Orthopaedic Hospital, founded by his father. He has remained to this day a great influence in her life.

Her mother gave her a sense of insecurity, and at six Eleanor felt apart from her brothers, Hall seated on her knee and Elliott.

When she was eight years old her mother died of diphtheria, and the death of her brother Elliott followed soon afterward.

Her father, who was an alcoholic, died shortly before her tenth birthday and Eleanor went to live with her grandmother at Tivoli. In the last letter her father ever wrote he asked: "How is your pony and the dogs at Tivoli, too?"

Franklin D. Roosevelt, her distant cousin, lived a few miles down the Hudson at Hyde Park. After they had danced together and talked at a children's party given by her uncle, Theodore Roosevelt, he told his mother: "Cousin Eleanor has a very good mind."

Eleanor Roosevelt at fifteen, just before she was sent to school in England by her grandmother for a European education. She had had an earnest, inquiring mind and had read every book she could lay her hands on in the big library at Tivoli. She was also beginning to think as shown by this essay on ambition.

Ambition

Some people consider ambition
sin but it seems to me to
a great good for it leads one to do
the things which without it one could nev
have been, look at Caesar it was
because he was ambitious that they k
him but would he ever have been
as great a man had he not had
ambition? would his name ever have
come down to us if he had not had
enough ambition to conquer the
would painters ever paint wonder
portraits or writers ever write
books if they did not have ambiti
Of course it is easier to have no
& just keep on the same way every
day & never ~~try~~ to do grand or great things
for it is only those who have ambition & who ~~try~~ who meet with diff

Jean de la Bruyère (1645-1696)

Jean de la Bruyère, né à Paris 1645, avocat au Parlement, fut chargé, sur la recommendation de Bossuet, d'enseigner l'histoire et la philosophie au petit-fils du grand Condé. Dans cette maison il vit le monde, étudia les hommes et écrivit ses **Caractères**. L'ouvrage parut en 1688, modestement présenté comme une traduction des anciens: **Les Caractères de Téophraste avec les caractères ou les mœurs de ce siècle.**

Philosophie de la Bruyère

La Bruyère n'a ni originalité ni profondeur comme philosophe. Il n'a que peu d'idées générales et celles sont celles de son temps. Il est spiritualiste comme Descartes et chrétien comme Bossuet; dans l'homme, il voit l'ambition, la vanité, l'hypocrisie; dans la femme une faiblesse d'intelligence incurable, une irrémédiable frivolité d'esprit et de cœur; dans la société un universel effort vers la jouissance des biens matériels et une universelle prosternation devant ceux qui possèdent la fortune; dans la vie, un immense déception, faite de désirs trompés qui deviennent des regrets et de regrets qui se transforment en de nouveaux désirs. C'est la philosophie d'un homme désabusé et, dans une certaine mesure, celle d'un célibataire morose, qui vit dans un monde qui le regarde d'en haut [illegible].

Les Sentiments

Les sentiments de La Bruyère sont plus profonds: il est doué d'une sensibilité inquiète et [illegible]. Comme certains pessimistes, sa philosophie

A French composition written while she was a student at Allenswood School near London, where . . .

. . . Mademoiselle Marie Souvestre was the headmistress. She had a great influence on the growing mind of her young American pupil.

She became proficient in Italian . . .

Dante Allighieri.

Dante Allighieri, che fu chiamato il padre della poesia italiana, nacque a Firenze nel 1265. Studiò le principale scienze e la teologia [illegible] Brunetto Latini. Studiò anche il disegno con Giotto sotto il celebre [illegible]mabue. Nel 1289, combattè contro i Ghibellini alla battaglia di Campal[illegible]. Più tardi fu mandato con degli altri ambasciatori, a Roma per [illegible]mandare a Bonifacio VIII di non mandare a Firenze come pacificatore [illegible] di Valois. Al suo ritorno seppe la notizia che era esiliato. Da quel [illegible]po vagava qua e là, sperando sempre che uno dei suoi potenti amici riuscirebbe a fare l'unità dell'Italia. È alla corte di Can Grande [illegible]la Scala che ha cominciato la Divina Commedia, e dedicò il [illegible]ma a quell'amico. Morì nel 1321 a Ravenna dove sono sepolte le [illegible]oglie.

Il Petrarca.

Francesco Petrarca nacque nel 1304 ad Arezzo [illegible] Petracco, notaio fiorentino, che era stato esiliato [illegible] Bianchi. Il padre vedendo l'ingegno di suo figlio, voleva

. . . and mastered German.

aus Blei gemacht, und Gutenberg, mit der Hilfe Peter[illegible] und Johann Faust fing eine Druckerei an in Mainz. Der Erzbischof Adolf von Nassau aber ~~Stadt~~ steckte die Stadt in Brand 1462, und die Leute, die das Geheimniss gekannten hatten, zogen in anderen Ländern, die die Druckerei verbreiteten.

Die Erfindung hatte sehr gute Folgen; jetzt konnte man auch Schulbücher haben, die Leute konnten lernen, Alle konnten eine [illegible] haben, und man konnte auch die größten [illegible] der Litteratur lesen.

16. S. 7. VII. 02

Ein Empfehlungs Brief

Sehr Geehrte Frau B..!

Als Antwort auf Ihren Brief kann ich Ihnen nur sagen, daß Fräulein S.. zehn Jahren bei mir gewesen ist und daß ich höchst zufrieden mit ihr bin.

Sie ist eine sehr gute Kinderzi[illegible]

Age of Dr. Johnson.

The importance of prose.
The age of philosophy
The influence of France
The rise of philosophical History
The rise of the modern novel. Sentimental & realistic.
The decadence of poetry.

Samuel Johnson 1709-1784.
London. 1738.
Vanity of Human Wishes 1749.
Irene. 1749
The Rambler & The Idler. 2 periodicals.
Dictionary 1755. (letter to Chesterfield)
Rasselas, prince of Abyssinia 1759.

The Rise of the Modern Novel.

The novelists. decline of the theatre & increase of reading public.

Richardson. The first novelist. The love stories of ordinary people.
Pamela 1740. or Virtue Rewarded
The novel of Sentiment & Sensibility - the analysis of the human heart.

Her favorite subject was English literature.

Mademoiselle Souvestre placed a high value on intellectual achievement, and in the three years the young girl spent under her guidance, Eleanor became an excellent scholar and regained some of the self-confidence she had lost when her father died.

During the three years she attended the Allenswood School, Eleanor Roosevelt (wearing wide-brimmed straw hat and seated in the second row at the far left) associated for the first time with young ladies of her own age. She was very popular and made many lasting friends.

Eleanor Roosevelt (third from the right in the last row) with the other members of her graduating class.

Loyalty and Friendship.

Loyalty is one of the few virtue
which most women lack, that is
why there are so few real friend-
ships among women for no friendship can exist without loyalty. With
a man it is a point of honor to be
loyal to his friend but a woman will
kiss her best friend one moment & when
she is gone will sit down with another
best friend & pick the other's character
to pieces. It may seem strange but no
matter how plain a woman may be
if truth & loyalty are stamped upon
her face all will be attracted to her
& she will do good to all who come near
her & those who know her will alway
love her for they will feel her loyal

She was beginning to observe her fellow human beings.

Terme de Mai à Juillet 1902.

		Zèle et Application.	Progrès.
Enseignement religieux			
Français	Langue	Elève excellente appliquée intelligente et [illegible]	
	Littérature M. Maître	Très bonne élève	Progrès très satisfaisants.
	Histoire		
Allemand R. Zwickel		Very industrious and conscientious pupil, very interested in the language and made remarkable progress	
Italien D. [illegible]		excellente élève — elle parle très facilement l'italien — élève regrettable et regrettée.	
Anglais	Langue		
	Littérature D. Strachey	Very good. Her progress was very marked this term	
	Histoire		
Mythologie			
Histoire générale			
Géographie			
Dessin et peinture			

		Zèle et Application.	Progrès.
Sciences exactes.	Arithmétique		
	Algèbre		
	Géométrie		
	Mécanique		
Latin			
Grec			
Musique	Piano M. [illegible]	An excellent worker.	Good.
	Violon [illegible]	has made very rapid progress	
	Harmonie		
	Chant		
Danse			
Travaux à l'aiguille R. Z.		Very industrious.	excellent progress.

Conduite: Elinor has had the most admirable influence on the school and gained the affection of many the respect of all. To me personally I feel I lose a dear friend in her
— Marie Souvestre

"Eleanor has had the most admirable influence on the school and gained the affection of many, the respect of all. To me personally I feel I lose a dear friend in her," wrote Mademoiselle Souvestre on the final report card.

On returning to America in 1902, she made her formal bow to New York society at an Assembly Ball.

THE ASSEMBLY BALL

The greatest social event of the season in New York, the first Assembly Ball, was held in the ball-room of the Waldorf-Astoria last week. Mrs. Astor and Mrs. Lloyd Brice were among those who received, and Mr. Elisha Dyer, Jr., led the cotillon

18	flowers & magazines for woman	1	25
	hansom	2	50
	Hall		50
	fee		50
19th	things for poor woman	5	
	stamps	2	
	hansom & fee	3	50
20th	hansom	2	50
	"	1	
		254	70

Since service to others had become a part of her character and society had taken on a larger meaning for her, Eleanor Roosevelt began to combine social activity with social work. She taught calisthenics and dancing at the Rivington Street Settlement House and worked with the Consumers' League investigating working conditions in garment factories. In an account book she kept at the time there is the listing—"things for poor woman $5."

She went to all the fashionable balls and parties and met many eligible young men, but her relatives wondered if she would ever attract any beaux.

And she did attract one beau . . .

. . . Franklin Roosevelt, who was then a senior at Harvard.

He is in the center gazing thoughtfully down at her. She visited his family home at Hyde Park. . .

. . . and at Campobello, their summer home.

In 1903, when Franklin was twenty-one and she was nineteen, they became engaged. "I have only a few bright prospects now," he said. "I have faith in you," she replied. "I'm sure you'll really amount to something someday."

His mother, Mrs. James Roosevelt, a strong-willed and dominating personality, was shocked when they told her, feeling that they were too young for marriage, and insisted that they wait a year before making an announcement. She then took her son out of Harvard and went with him on a cruise to the West Indies, hoping he would change his mind.

Eleanor Roosevelt in her wedding gown.

In the Name of the Father, and of the Son, and of the Holy Ghost, Amen.

Diocese of New York.

Church of the Incarnation,
New York City.

+

This is to Certify

That Franklin Delano Roosevelt

and Eleanor Roosevelt

were united in

Holy Matrimony

According to the Rite of the Protestant Episcopal Church in the United States of America, and the Laws of the State of New York, on this Seventeenth day of March A.D. 1905.

Endicott Peabody
Rector.

Witnesses.

Theodore Roosevelt
Edith Kermit Roosevelt

What therefore God hath joined together let not man put asunder.—St. Mark x. 9.

The marriage ceremony was performed by Dr. Endicott Peabody, headmaster of Groton School, which Franklin had attended.

The President Gives Away His Niece Eleanor in Marriage.

Mr. and Mrs. Roosevelt Attend the Wedding of His Late Brother's Daughter and Franklin Delano Roosevelt.

Cheers from East Seventy-sixth street at 3.30 o'clock sounded the approach of President Roosevelt, whose presence at the wedding of his niece, Miss Eleanor Roosevelt, and Franklin Delano Roosevelt, almost made the bride a secondary consideration. This wedding was celebrated in the twin homes of Mrs. Henry Parrish, jr., and Mrs. E. Livingston Ludlow, Nos. 6 and 8 East Seventy-sixth street.

Owing to the immense crowds that surrounded these houses the entire block was closed and seventy-five policemen were employed to keep order. Although the invitations were distributed sparingly, it seemed as if there had been no regrets, and the crush inside was so great that many guests did not get beyond the threshold of the drawing-room.

When the open landau stopped in front of the awning women at neighboring windows cheered and waved handkerchiefs. The President half arose from his seat and waved his silk hat. But the President's smile was not so expansive before he entered the house as when he reappeared, and when he gave away his only brother's daughter his face wore an unusually solemn expression.

Women Crowd to See Him.

While the wedding of the Roosevelt cousins was of interest to the fashionable set, Miss Roosevelt's uncle was the leading attraction, and so eager was the public to catch a glimpse of him that at noon little knots of women took their stand in East Seventy-sixth street and made themselves at home on the steps of the Temple Beth-El, at the Fifth avenue corner.

At 2 o'clock these women were dislodged by the police and Seventy-sixth street was cleared completely.

By this time the bridesmaids were arriving. The floral decorations in the two houses were pink and green, and the ceilings of the reception halls were hung with Southern smilax and baskets of pink roses.

The partition between the Ludlow and Parish houses had been removed for the wedding, and the double drawing-room formed a large enough space for the guests. These rooms were modestly touched with flowers and at the lower end an altar was fitted up with a background of palms. The cousins were married under an enormous bouquet of pink roses, containing 450 flowers.

Miss Roosevelt was attended by Miss Alice Roosevelt, Miss Ellen Delano, Miss Muriel Robbins, Miss Isabella Selmes, Miss Corrine Robinson and Miss Helen Cutting. Lathrop Brown acted as best man, as the bridegroom's half brother, J. Roosevelt Roosevelt, was ill. The ushers were: Nicholas Biddle, Owen Winston, Lyman Delano, Warren Robbins, Charles B. Bradley and Thomas Beal.

Miss Roosevelt walked down the improvised aisle with the President. The bride's gown was white satin with a court train and a trimming of lace. The lace veil was an heirloom. The bride was lavishly jewelled. She wore a dog collar of pearls, a diamond bowknot and the veil was fastened with a diamond crescent, which had been worn by the late Mrs. Elliot Roosevelt.

The Rev. Mr. Endicott Peabody, of Groton, Mass., married the pair.

President Wears the Green.

The President's arrival was well timed, and his mounted escort moved slowly toward the Parish house at 3.30 to the moment. With the President in the landau were Mrs. Roosevelt, little Miss Ethel Roosevelt and Secretary Loeb.

A huge bunch of genuine shamrock hung in the President's button-hole and, although the leaves looked sadly withered, he continued to wear them.

Besides the mounted police, the President had a bodyguard of six Secret Service men, who did not leave his side until he was well within the Parish house.

Mrs. Valentine Hall, the bride's grandmother, in whose names the invitations were issued, sent out two different cards. Some of the guests were asked only for the reception. Mr. and Mrs. Charles B. Alexander were among the reception guests, and when they arrived too early they sat on a vacant stoop near by to wait. Finally one of the Parish servants asked them to come in.

At 5 o'clock the Roosevelt party was ready to leave. The carriage turned toward Fifth avenue from Seventy-sixth street. At one corner a vacant lot is screened by a tall fence, and the top of this fence was black with small boys. From them the President received three cheers, and the President tipped his hat to them. "Three cheers for Teddy! Ain't he the real thing?" came from a hundred youthful throats, and then the President shook his fist playfully at the boys. In his excitement one small youth fell backward.

It was a swift ride down to the home of Mrs. Elizabeth Roosevelt, No. 4 West Fifty-seventh street, where the President and Mrs. Roosevelt are stopping.

At the Roosevelt-Roosevelt wedding the following families were represented: The Burdens, the Sloanes, the Vanderbilts, the Baylieses, the Bradish Johnsons, the Chanlers, the Winthrops, the Riggses, the Alexanders, the Mortimers, the Belmonts, the Crugers and the Van Rensselaers.

President Theodore Roosevelt gave his niece away.

The newlyweds went on a European honeymoon the following summer and Franklin Roosevelt, a good amateur photographer, took pictures on their honeymoon. Later he bound them in an album which he hand-lettered and gave to his bride as a Christmas present.

The bride took this picture.

At Assynt

Venezia
The Last Day

2. The Young Wife

When Franklin and Eleanor Roosevelt returned from their European honeymoon in the fall of 1905, they moved into a house at 125 East Thirty-sixth Street in New York City. It had been rented by Mrs. James Roosevelt, who had also furnished it and engaged the necessary servants. While her husband continued his law studies at Columbia, Eleanor Roosevelt led the conventional life of a young society matron, entertaining and being entertained, having and bringing up children, caring for a busy and increasing household. After the insecurity of her early years it was a peaceful and pleasant existence, dominated by her husband and her mother-in-law and their way of life.

Their first child, Anna Eleanor, was born on May 3, 1906, and the second, James, on December 23, 1907. After James's birth, Mrs. Roosevelt, at the urging of her mother-in-law and a cousin, gave up her social-service work. They felt that she might bring diseases home to her own children by visiting slum sections. "The biggest and most beautiful of all babies" was born on March 18, 1909, but died the following November after an attack of influenza.

The young Roosevelts were then living in a new house at 49 East Sixty-fifth Street which Mrs. James Roosevelt had built for them. It adjoined her own home and there were connecting doors between the two buildings. Here again Mrs. James Roosevelt had taken care of the furnishings and engaged the servants as she had done for her daughter-in-law in the Thirty-sixth Street house. All her life Eleanor Roosevelt had lived in the homes of others—first with her grandmother Hall and now with her mother-in-law—and as time went on she began to feel a deep need for a place that she could feel really belonged to her. Shortly after moving into the Sixty-fifth Street house, Franklin Roosevelt returned home from his law office and found his young wife seated beside her dressing table, sobbing uncontrollably. Self-control had become one of the strongest facets of Eleanor Roosevelt's character, and he was bewildered by the sight of her tears. When he asked her why she was crying, she revealed to him for the first time her discontent at not having a home of her own, one that she herself had planned and arranged according to her own tastes and desires. He gently told her that he thought she was "quite mad" and assured her that she would feel differently about her new home after she had lived in it for a while. Trained to do what was expected of her, she accepted her new surroundings as she had accepted the life that had been planned for her.

Her fourth child, Elliott, was born on September 23, 1910, and that same year her husband made his first bid for political office. He ran for New York State senator in a district which had not elected a Democrat in thirty-two years. When he won, one of his supporters, Thomas Lynch of Poughkeepsie, made the prediction that one day Franklin D. Roosevelt would be the president of the United States. To back up his belief, Mr. Lynch stored away two bottles of champagne for a celebration when his prophecy came to pass.

On New Year's Day in 1911 the family moved to Albany, New York, and for the first time Eleanor Roosevelt had a home of her own. It was a rented one, to be sure, and in a sense she had to share it with Franklin Roosevelt's political associates, but that was quite agreeable to her, since she firmly believed that it was a wife's duty to share her husband's life and to help his career in every possible way. That belief was tested shortly after her arrival in Albany when her husband assumed the leadership in a fight against Tammany Hall's candidate for United States senator—at that time senators were picked by the state legislature.

Thirty legislators supported State Senator Roosevelt's stand, but they lacked a meeting place where they could carry on their discussions and plot their strategy without being overheard by newspaper reporters or Tammany spies. Realizing that the legislators were away from their own homes, Eleanor Roosevelt invited them to come to her house at the end of the legislative day, and for several weeks the Roosevelt living room was turned into a political meeting hall. When the discussions became heated and the noise and cigar smoke disturbed the children, she simply moved the nursery to an upper floor. When the sessions, which often lasted until well after midnight, broke up, Mrs. Roosevelt served the men sandwiches and beer.

Roosevelt won his fight against Tammany and gave his wife credit for helpfulness in his first important political test when he later said, "That was the beginning of my wife's political sagacity and cooperation."

In the summer of 1912, when he was up for re-election, Franklin Roosevelt caught typhoid fever and had to place his campaign and his hope of winning again in the hands of a former Albany newspaperman named Louis McHenry Howe. Howe was an unprepossessing, gnomelike person with a pock-marked face whom Mrs. James Roosevelt openly disliked and her daughter-in-law considered an unpleasant little man. But Howe was driven by a belief in Franklin D. Roosevelt's destiny that neither dislike nor disapproval could ever shake.

"I was as determined that I would not like him as he was that I should," Mrs. Roosevelt said after Howe's death in 1936. "He came and sat in Franklin's room [while he was recuperating from typhoid fever] and I thoroughly disapproved of all the cigarettes he smoked and could not understand that he was winning my husband's campaign. I could not see what Franklin saw in him, nor why everyone thought him such a political genius. But he kept on coming to my desk and talking to me, day after day, until I became interested, in spite of myself, and eventually I realized how much he had to offer, and was glad to have his advice and friendship."

Through Howe's skillful planning and hard work the bedridden candidate was re-elected, despite the opposition of Tammany Hall and the Republican party.

In the spring of 1913 President Wilson appointed Franklin Roosevelt Assistant Secretary of the Navy, and Franklin took Howe with him as his assistant. Mrs. Roosevelt and her family then made another move, this time to Washington, D. C.

While her husband was busy with his new job, she made the myriad social calls the wife of a member of "The Little Cabinet" must make, managed her home, looked after her children, and still found time to study shorthand and typing and take cooking lessons.

The fifth child, Franklin D. Roosevelt, Jr., was born on August 17, 1914, and her last, John Aspinwall, on March 16, 1916.

When America entered the war in 1917, Eleanor Roosevelt,

who then had a family of five children, became extremely active in war work. With Mrs. Josephus Daniels she organized a Red Cross canteen. Three days a week she worked in the kitchen of the Red Cross canteen, making sandwiches for the soldiers passing through the capital on troop trains. Once she cut her finger to the bone in a bread-slicing machine but kept right on with her job, tying a handkerchief around the torn finger. When she returned home, the family doctor, who had been called, told her it was too late to stitch the cut and she still carries the scar. One day a week she distributed wool for the knitting of sweaters and helmets and checked in the finished articles completed by volunteer workers. Every week she visited the Navy Hospital with cigarettes and other gifts and talked to the sick sailors, doing what she could to help them. She also visited shell-shocked sailors who were placed in one wing of St. Elizabeth's, the government's hospital for the insane. On one such visit she was appalled by the dreadful conditions under which demented patients had to live and sent a report to the Secretary of the Interior, who had jurisdiction over the hospital. This marked her first attempt to improve a government institution. As a result of her efforts, Congress appropriated more money for St. Elizabeth's, which soon became a model institution for the insane.

Immediately after the Armistice, Assistant Secretary Roosevelt was assigned to France on navy business and his wife insisted on accompanying him—despite objections of the State Department—since he had not yet recovered from attacks of pneumonia and influenza. She toured the battlefronts only a few weeks after the war ended, and visited our wounded soldiers in army hospitals.

Early in 1919 the Roosevelts returned to America with President Wilson's party. They both shared his high hopes for the new League of Nations, which promised to prevent future wars. At lunch one day during that trip, President Wilson in speaking of the League told the young Roosevelts, "The United States must go in, or it will break the heart of the world . . ." but it was his own heart that was broken after his valiant but vain attempt to win approval for this international peace organization.

After the war the Roosevelts were once again able to enjoy to the fullest the life with their children. At Hyde Park and Campobello they went on picnics with them, played games, took them on sailing trips, and led a close and happy family life. In the summer of 1920, however, this pleasant routine was interrupted when Mrs. Roosevelt, who was staying with the children at Campobello while her husband attended the Democratic convention in San Francisco, received a telegram from the Secretary of the Navy telling her that her husband had been unanimously nominated for vice-president to run with James M. Cox.

She accompanied her husband on a whistle-stop tour of the country as the only woman in his private car, and her political education began in earnest. Fighting her shyness, she stood on the rear platform with her husband when the train stopped at various towns, listened as he spoke, waved at the crowd who came to see him, shook thousands of hands, met and talked with political leaders along the way, attended Democratic rallies, learned that politics was composed of idealists as well as rogues, and became for the first time, in a tentative way, Franklin D. Roosevelt's partner in public as well as private life. As the campaign train sped across the country she listened to strategy discussions reminiscent of the meetings held in her Albany home ten years before. While the campaign staff, which included Thomas Lynch, who had predicted Franklin D. Roosevelt would one day be president, relaxed by playing cards, she went over speeches at the insistence of Louis Howe, who was constantly prodding her to take a greater interest in politics.

After the defeat of Cox and Roosevelt, she finally decided to take an active part in politics and became a board member of the New York State League of Women Voters. Having kept the promise she had made herself while on her honeymoon in Scotland, she now had an excellent knowledge of how the United States government was run and she accepted the responsibility of reporting on national legislation for the new women's political organization.

Following the overwhelming Republican victory, Franklin Roosevelt returned to private law practice, but in a letter to Steve Early, who had been his press aide during the 1920 campaign, he sounded this optimistic note—"Thank the Lord we are both comparatively youthful."

The great turning point in his career did not occur at Washington or Albany but on the tiny island of Campobello in the summer of 1921. On a hot August day Franklin Roosevelt had helped fight a forest fire, then went for a swim in the cold waters of the Bay of Fundy. That evening he complained of a chill, and the next morning he had a high fever. Two days later his legs became paralyzed and the local doctor did not know the cause. Deeply alarmed, Eleanor Roosevelt telephoned Louis Howe at his home in Massachusetts and, when he learned what had happened, he took the next train to Campobello. There were no nurses on the island and, as her husband's condition became worse, Mrs. Roosevelt watched over him day and night, sleeping on a cot in his room. She and Louis Howe took turns massaging the sick man's legs in an effort to restore the circulation in his paralyzed legs. Finally a specialist arrived and, after a thorough examination, told her that her husband had infantile paralysis and might never walk again.

When the doctors decided it was safe to move Franklin Roosevelt to a New York hospital, the sick man was placed in the bottom of a boat and when it arrived at Eastport, Maine, he was transferred to a train in the greatest secrecy so as to avoid the questions of newspaper reporters.

Eleanor Roosevelt and Louis Howe rode on the train with the crippled man. This time when it stopped along the way there were no cheering crowds, no outstretched hands to be shaken, no speeches. Perhaps, as the train sped through the night, two speeches that she and Franklin had exchanged a long time ago came to Eleanor Roosevelt's mind:

"I have only a few bright prospects now."

"I have faith in you. I'm sure you'll really amount to something someday."

When the train pulled into the station in New York City bearing the stricken Franklin D. Roosevelt, Thomas Lynch of Poughkeepsie, who in 1910 had stored away two bottles of champagne for a celebration, was waiting on the platform to help an anguished wife get her husband to a hospital.

Eleanor Roosevelt on returning from her honeymoon led the life of a conventional young society matron.

Mrs. James Roosevelt built a home for her son and his wife at 49 East Sixty-fifth Street (center) in New York City. It adjoined her own home, and there were connecting doors between the two buildings. Mrs. Roosevelt also furnished the house and engaged the servants for her daughter-in-law.

Mrs. James Roosevelt's home at Hyde Park on the Hudson River . . .

. . . where the young couple spent many holidays.

Mrs. James Roosevelt's cottage at Campobello, a small Canadian island off the coast of Maine, where Eleanor and her husband joined her for the summer.

When they were at Campobello, Franklin, who was an excellent sailor, loved to take his family and friends sailing in the Bay of Fundy and the Atlantic.

Eleanor Roosevelt, who had always lived in other people's homes—first with her grandmother and now with her mother-in-law—began to feel a deep need for a place of her own and a way of life that she, herself, had planned.

But duty had become her motivating force, and she accepted the way of life of her husband and mother-in-law.

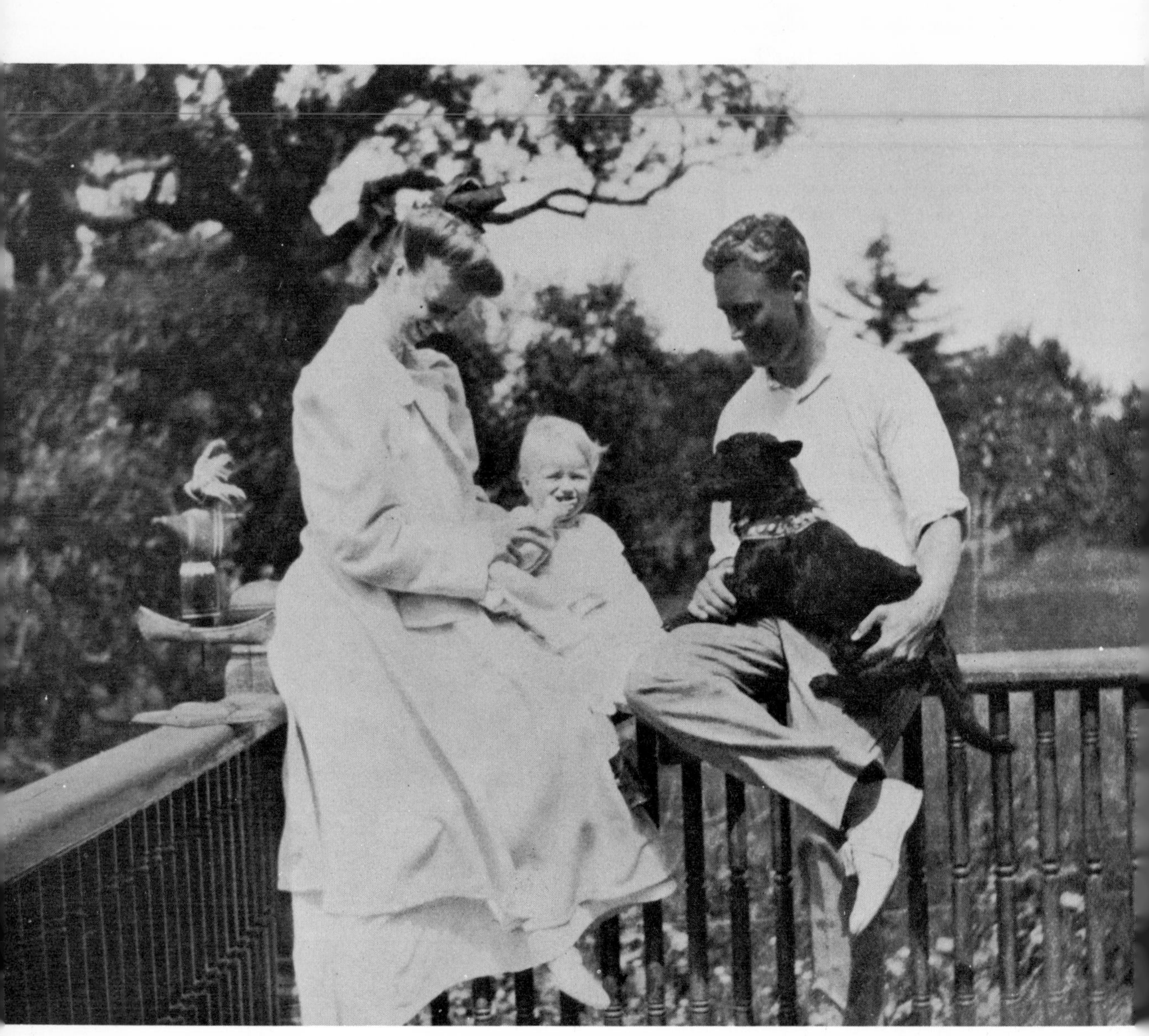

Eleanor and Franklin Roosevelt with their first child, Anna Eleanor, born in 1907. The dog, Duffy, was the first in a long line of Scotties in the Roosevelt family.

In 1910 Franklin Roosevelt made his first bid for political office and was elected New York State Senator in a district that had not supported a Democrat in thirty-two years. His wife stands behind him as he greets voters.

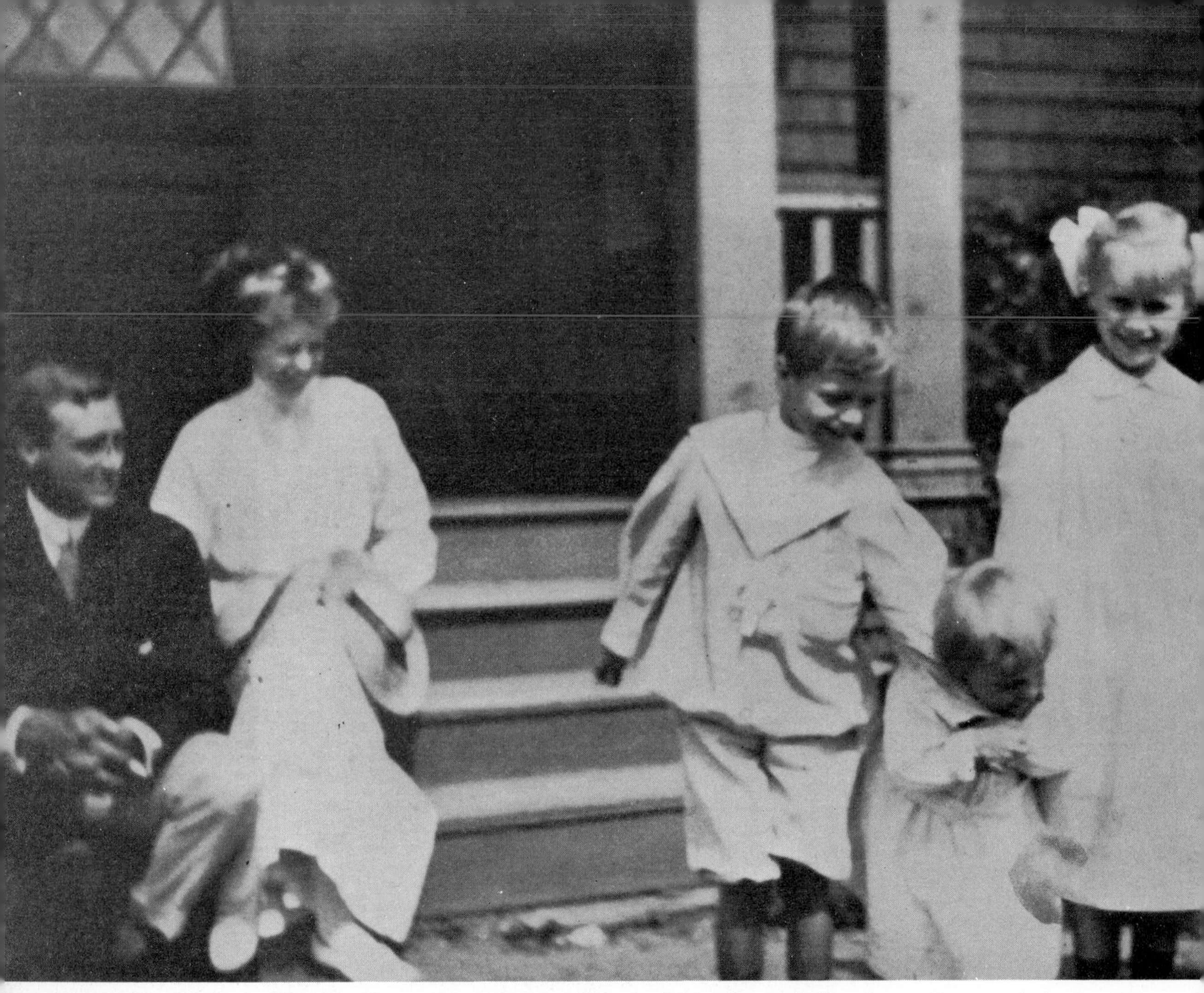

A growing family accompanies the Roosevelts to Campobello, Anna, James, their first boy, and Elliott the baby.

President Woodrow Wilson appointed Franklin D. Roosevelt Assistant Secretary of the Navy in 1913. His wife went with him on his first inspection tour of a navy yard.

In Washington Franklin Roosevelt had to step lively to keep up with his Navy duties.

Mrs. Roosevelt made the many social calls a wife of a member of "The Little Cabinet" must make, ran her household, looked after her children, entertained, and still found time to study shorthand and typing and to take cooking lessons.

When America entered the war in 1917, Eleanor Roosevelt became a leader in Washington war work. With Mrs. Josephus Daniels she organized a Red Cross canteen and superintended a corps of volunteers. When her husband was assigned to France on navy business immediately after the Armistice, she insisted on going with him, despite the objections of the State Department, since he had not yet recovered from attacks of pneumonia and influenza. She toured the battlefronts only a few weeks after the war ended. She is shown with her husband in front of the ruins of St. Quentin Cathedral.

The young Roosevelts returned to America in early January, 1919, aboard the S. S. *Aztec* with President Wilson's party.

Franklin D. Roosevelt and his wife shared President Wilson's high hopes for the new League of Nations, which promised to prevent future wars . . .

. . . and both hoped that the war which had just ended in victory would be the last they would ever see.

Freed from the outside pressures of the war, family life is resumed again . . .

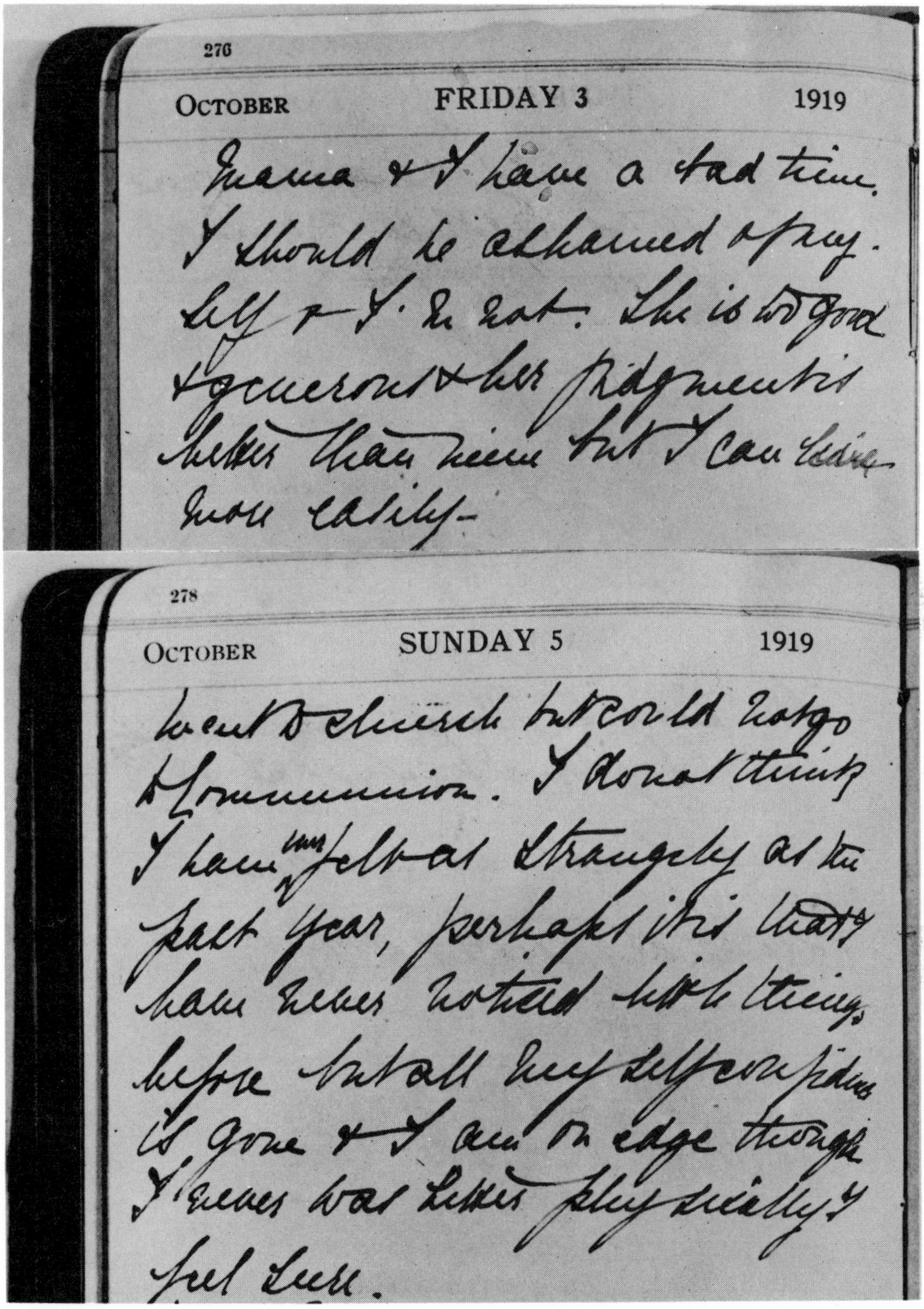

276

OCTOBER FRIDAY 3 1919

Mama & I have a bad time. I should be ashamed of myself & I am not. She is so good & generous & her judgment is better than mine but I can leave more easily.

278

OCTOBER SUNDAY 5 1919

Went to church but could not go to Communion. I do not think I have ever felt as strangely as this past year, perhaps it is that I have never noticed little things before but all my self confidence is gone & I am on edge though I never was better physically & feel well.

. . . and there was an undercurrent of struggle with her mother-in-law, whom she so much admired.

There were now five children—Franklin, Jr., on his father's knee, was born on August 17, 1914, and John Aspinwall, held by his mother, the last child, on March 16, 1916.

July 8-1920

THE WHITE HOUSE
WASHINGTON

My dear Mrs. Roosevelt:
Knowing how overwhelmed you will be with letters I have hesitated to add to the burden - but cannot resist this little personal word to send our hearty good wishes and hope for success in November.
Faithfully yours
Edith Bolling Wilson

GOVERNMENT TELEGRAPH SERVICE,
DEPARTMENT OF PUBLIC WORKS,
DOMINION OF CANADA.

Form No. 2.

The following message was received by the Government for transmission, subject to the terms and conditions printed on the blank form No. 1, which terms and conditions have been agreed to by the sender.

D. H. KEELEY, *General Superintendent.*

Sent by ______ Received by ______ Time 1 P.M. Check 17

No. 15 Dated Washington D.C. July 7 1920

Received at

To Mrs Franklin Roosevelt -
Welshpool NB

Papers are demanding your picture. Is there one at the house here that I can have copied?
Howe

Sending special messenger on account of this one asking an answer —

The smooth and pleasant routine of family life was interrupted early in the summer of 1920 when Eleanor Roosevelt, who was staying with the children at Campobello while her husband attended the Democratic Convention in San Francisco, received a telegram telling her that Franklin D. Roosevelt had been unanimously nominated vice-president to run with James M. Cox.

Franklin Roosevelt delivered his acceptance speech at his Hyde Park home while his wife (in left background) and his mother (seated directly behind him) listen. It was the first big meeting held at Hyde Park.

Eleanor Roosevelt traveled with her husband on his whistle-stop campaign tour of the country as the only woman in his private car. On the extreme left is Louis McHenry Howe, who had been FDR's political adviser since 1910. Beside him is Thomas Lynch, of Poughkeepsie, who ten years before predicted Franklin D. Roosevelt would be president.

James M. Cox and Franklin D. Roosevelt leading a political parade during the 1920 campaign.

Mrs. Cox and Mrs. Roosevelt watch their husbands from a reviewing stand.

Before the election . . .

. . . after the election.

Following his defeat in 1920, Franklin D. Roosevelt returned to his private law practice and spent more time with his growing family at Campobello.

The great turning point in the career of Franklin D. Roosevelt and in the life of his wife occurred on a hot August day in 1921 at Campobello. He had helped fight a forest fire, then went for a swim in the cold waters of the Bay of Fundy. That night he had a chill, and the next morning his fever was high. Two days later his legs became paralyzed.

his feet [illegible]. I dread the
time when I have to tell Franklin
& it wrings my heart for it is

all so much worse to a man than
to a woman but the 3 doctors
agree he will be eventually _well_
if nothing unfavourable happens
in the next ten days or so & at
present all signs are favourable
so we should be very thankful.
Much love
Eleanor
Aug 18th

The anguished wife wrote a letter to a relative: "I dread the time when I have to tell Franklin & it wrings my heart for it is all so much worse to a man than to a woman but the 3 doctors agree he will be eventually *well* if nothing unfavourable happens in the next ten days or so & at present all signs are favourable so we should be very thankful.

Much love,
Eleanor."

A stricken wife faces the future. . . . There were no nurses on Campobello, and Eleanor Roosevelt exhausted herself taking care of her crippled husband. She stayed with him day and night, sleeping on a cot in his room. Finally, a specialist arrived and told her that her husband had infantile paralysis.

3. The Public Figure

Franklin D. Roosevelt spent three months in a New York City hospital after his attack of infantile paralysis in the summer of 1921, then began a long, slow struggle to regain his health and the use of his limbs. As he went through this personal ordeal, another struggle was going on around him that would have great bearing on his future life and career. The contestants were two well-bred ladies, shy and submissive Eleanor Roosevelt and her forceful mother-in-law.

His mother had decided that her crippled son should give up his law practice and politics and retire to Hyde Park and live the life of a country squire like his father before him. His wife was convinced that his recovery would be hastened if he continued to take an interest in the world around him and continued to see his many friends and political associates.

"My mother-in-law was a woman of great character," Mrs. Roosevelt once observed. "She always knew what was right and wrong. She was kind and generous and loyal to the family through thick and thin. But it was hard to differ with her. She never gave up an idea, whether it was for herself or for you. And her methods of achieving her own ends at times seemed a bit ruthless if you were not in accord. She dominated me for years.

"His illness finally made me stand on my own two feet in regard to my husband's life, my own life, and my children's training. The alternative would have been to become a completely colorless echo of my husband and mother-in-law and torn between them. I might have stayed a weak character forever if I had not found that out."

On the surface the struggle between the two women was a polite one without harsh words or recriminations and neither ever lost her temper.

"In all the years I only lost my temper with Mother-in-law once and that was over the training of the children," said Mrs. Roosevelt. "I made up my mind then that I would never lose it again. She forgot all about it the next day, but I have remembered it all my life."

The conflict over how crippled Franklin D. Roosevelt and his family should lead their lives reached a climax early in 1922 when the two women called on Dr. George Draper.

"Dr. Draper, I'm sure you will agree with me that Franklin will be an invalid for the rest of his life," began Mrs. James Roosevelt. "He should, therefore, be retired to a wheel chair. Every precaution should be taken to protect him from excitement and overstimulation."

"I know my husband well enough to feel that this would be the worst thing you could do to him," said Eleanor Roosevelt. "He is not an invalid. A renewed interest in life is what he needs. Association with his friends and as much activity as he can stand as his strength comes back will be the best thing in the world for him."

"I ought to know what is best for my only son," said his mother. "These political friends of his will sap his strength. He needs rest and complete quiet."

"We must do what you think best, Dr. Draper," said Eleanor Roosevelt, "but believe me, if you relegate my husband to the wheel chair now, and forbid him the interests he needs to stimulate his mind, you will be making him an invalid for life. If he fights, he may overcome his handicap."

Dr. Draper meditated for a few moments, then addressing Eleanor Roosevelt, said: "You're right, his recovery will be speeded if he takes part in public affairs again. You can do many of the heavier tasks for him. But he is not an invalid and there is no reason why he should be treated as one."

And as Franklin D. Roosevelt fought to overcome his handicap, his wife never treated him as an invalid. In a few months he could crawl along the floor and play games with his younger sons, who were forgetting that their father had ever been ill.

The "heavier tasks" Dr. Draper had mentioned included some of the responsibilities of a father. Eleanor had abandoned horseback riding after a frightening experience but took it up again and learned how to swim so that she could teach her children. She learned to play athletic games with them and, finding out how to pitch a tent and paddle a canoe, she took the two younger boys on camping trips.

In order to make certain that her husband would take part in public affairs she invited Louis Howe to stay in their home and cooperated with him in keeping Franklin D. Roosevelt interested in politics and in his political career. And starting in 1922, Eleanor Roosevelt became more and more active in politics. When under strain she had a habit of giggling nervously and she was terrified of speaking in public but, under the prodding of Howe, she accepted an invitation to preside at a fund-raising luncheon of Democratic women and made her first political speech. At that meeting she met Nancy Cook, who was organizing Democratic women in New York State, Marion Dickerman, a schoolteacher who had run for assemblywoman from Oswego against a Republican opposed to social legislation proposed by women, and Caroline O'Day, later one of the first women elected to Congress. These three women now became her close friends and political associates, and she often invited them to Hyde Park, where they discussed their ideas and aims with Franklin D. Roosevelt.

With Howe's help she edited the *Women's Democratic News* and worked regularly at the New York State Democratic headquarters doing whatever there was to do from licking stamps to raising badly needed funds. During the next two years she visited every county in New York State organizing women's groups and campaigning for equal opportunity for women in the Democratic party.

Once when she and another volunteer worker called on a county chairman in the southern part of the state, his wife told them that he was not at home. "All right," said Mrs. Roosevelt, who knew that the chairman was opposed to women in politics and had reason to think that he was really inside his home, "we will just sit here on the steps until he comes." They sat down and after an hour of waiting the wife reappeared and told them that she had no idea when her husband would return. "It doesn't matter," said Mrs. Roosevelt with a smile. "We have nothing else to do. We will wait." Eventually the chairman, looking embarrassed, came out on the porch and talked to them.

Although Franklin D. Roosevelt was unable to walk, he was again leading a normal life, attending to his law practice, and gradually resuming an active role in politics. In 1924 he ran Governor Alfred E. Smith's pre-convention campaign, and using crutches for the first time, he walked onto the speaker's platform in Madison Square Garden and made his memorable nominating speech for "The Happy Warrior."

The New York *Herald Tribune* made this comment: "From the time Roosevelt made his speech in nominating Smith, which was the one great speech of the convention, he has been easily the foremost figure on the floor or the platform."

And the *Evening World* paid him a tribute that might have been written by Eleanor Roosevelt herself:

> Whether Governor Smith wins or loses, Franklin D. Roosevelt stands out as the real hero of the Democratic Convention of 1924. Adversity has lifted him above the bickering, the religious bigotry, conflicting personal ambition, and petty sectional prejudices. It has made him the one leader commanding the respect and admiration of delegations from all sections of the land. . . . Roosevelt might be a pathetic, tragic figure but for the fine courage that flashes in his smile. . . . It holds observers enchained.

Smith, after being deadlocked with William G. McAdoo for a hundred ballots, finally lost to John W. Davis of West Virginia, a compromise candidate. Eleanor Roosevelt campaigned in New York State for Davis. She devised a campaign car with a large teapot on the top, to dramatize the Teapot Dome scandals during the Harding administration, and toured with it through every county in the state.

In the years that followed, Mrs. Roosevelt not only continued her political work, but added two new activities. In 1926 she went into partnership with Miss Cook and Miss Dickerman and founded a furniture factory in Hyde Park to provide employment for young farmers in the winter months. In 1927 she again joined forces with the same two friends and purchased the Todhunter School for girls in New York City. Miss Dickerman became the principal and Eleanor Roosevelt was the vice-principal. She had always had a desire to teach, and she now conducted classes in English literature and civics.

In addition to her political activities, school work, writing, and business commitments, she also managed her New York City home and superintended her younger sons' education so that when her first grandchild, Anna Eleanor Dall (Sistie), was born on March 25, 1927, she was undoubtedly the busiest grandmother in the United States.

In January of 1929 she moved her family into another house—the Executive Mansion at Albany, New York—and assumed a new role as a governor's lady. While fulfilling her official duties as Governor Roosevelt's wife, she continued to teach at Todhunter School, commuting between Albany and New York City, kept an eye on her furniture factory, wrote editorials for the *Women's Democratic News*, made her first airplane trip, spoke at scores of political meetings, took Franklin, Jr., and John on a European tour, broadcast regularly over the radio, edited a magazine called *Babies, Just Babies*, became the grandmother of two more children, and began to create an American legend of free and energetic enterprise.

She also continued to be her husband's eyes, ears, and legs. When Governor Roosevelt visited state institutions, he would ask her to inspect the inside of a building while he was being driven around the grounds. He would question her in the greatest of detail about what she had observed. Once, when he asked her if she had investigated a seemingly insignificant item, she replied, "Why, I didn't look at that." "Well, you'd better look," he replied.

"It was he who taught me to observe," Mrs. Roosevelt has since reported. "Just sitting with him in the observation car of a train I learned how to watch the tracks and see their condition, how to look at the countryside and note whether there was soil erosion, and what condition the forests and fields were in, and as we went through the outskirts of a town or village, I soon learned to look at the clothes on the washlines and at the cars, and to notice whether houses needed painting. Little by little I found I was able to answer my husband's questions after I had taken a trip alone and given him the information he would have gathered had he taken the trip himself. . . . It was the best education I ever had."

Governor Roosevelt based many of his plans, reforms, and decisions on information supplied him by his wife, and he frequently used the term "Eleanor and I" when discussing issues, new and needed legislation, and future plans with his aides and associates. The Roosevelts had become a well-coordinated team.

When Franklin D. Roosevelt was nominated for the presidency in 1932, the organization methods and campaign techniques which had been carefully worked out over the years by Eleanor Roosevelt and her associates in the Women's Division of the New York State Democratic Committee were extended to all the other states, and these provided Roosevelt with substantial support by women's groups during his campaign.

On election night, when President Hoover conceded defeat, Eleanor Roosevelt, who had a lifelong aversion to alcohol based on what overindulgence had done to members of her own family, broke one of her rules of self-discipline and sipped from a paper cup filled with champagne which had been carefully hoarded for twenty-two years by Thomas Lynch of Poughkeepsie for just such a celebration.

Then in March of 1933, Eleanor Roosevelt, who had never lived in a home of her own, moved into another that belonged to others—the people of the United States.

As Franklin D. Roosevelt fought to regain his health after an attack of infantile paralysis, a struggle began between two well-bred ladies, his submissive wife and his forceful mother, that would decide his future career. Eleanor Roosevelt felt that her husband's recovery would be speeded if he kept active in politics.

His mother insisted that her son's political friends would sap his strength, and decided that he should retire to Hyde Park and live the life of a country squire as had his father before him.

Eleanor Roosevelt won, and at the 1924 Democratic Convention FDR, using crutches for the first time, walked onto the platform at Madison Square Garden and nominated Al Smith as "the Happy Warrior." (Son James holds crutches at extreme left.)

Eleanor Roosevelt, who had worked closely with Louis McHenry Howe (seated opposite her) since 1921 to keep her husband interested in politics and his political career, had now become an important leader in the Women's Division of the Democratic party and took an active part in the 1924 campaign, visiting every county in New York State to organize women's groups.

She also had to assume some of the responsibilities of a father. She learned to swim so that she could teach her children. She is on the right in the upper picture, and John W. Davis, presidential candidate, stands behind her. She took her family on their vacations to Campobello.

She learned to pitch a tent and paddle a canoe and took her two younger sons on camping trips. And she saw to it that leading figures in the Women's Division of the Democratic party met informally with her husband.

FDR's six-room cottage at Warm Springs, Georgia, where he frequently went for his health.

The warm, medicinal waters helped him regain the use of his limbs and he spent much of his time swimming.

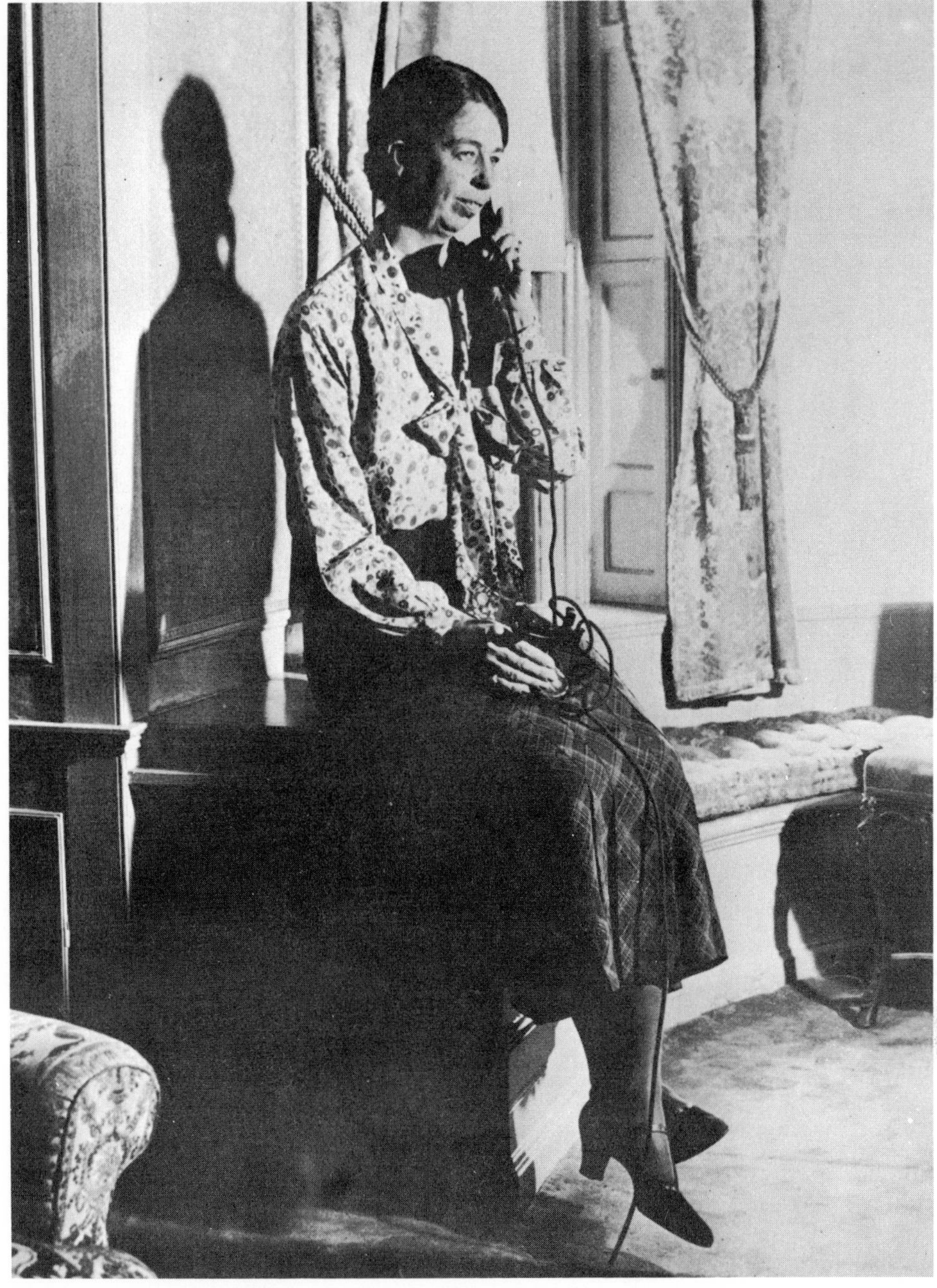

He was at Warm Springs in 1928 when Eleanor Roosevelt, the only person who could get him to come to the phone, called him and then put Al Smith on the wire. Smith persuaded him to run for governor.

GOVERNOR FRANKLIN D. ROOSEVELT AND HIS WIFE, LEAVING THEIR FIRST CHU
SERVICE AFTER THEIR ARRIVAL IN ALBANY, WHEN MR. ROOSEVELT WAS M
GOVERNOR

FDR receiving congratulations at the Governor's Inaugural Ball in Albany in 1929. Standing behind him are the two people responsible for his once again becoming an important public figure, his wife and Louis McHenry Howe.

Governor and Mrs. Roosevelt in the Executive Mansion at Albany.

Mrs. Roosevelt gets to know her new neighbors, who call on her at the State Mansion.

She regularly attended sessions of the New York legislature, and her husband frequently used the term "Eleanor and I" when discussing issues and new and necessary laws with his aides and associates.

She christened the Governor's airplane, then took her first airplane ride.

The first grandchild, Anna Eleanor Dall (Sistie), daughter of Anna (right), joins the family group.

In 1929 Mrs. Roosevelt with her friend and associate Marion Dickerman took her younger sons, Franklin, Jr., and John, on the grand tour of Europe, as part of their education.

At Hyde Park, where unemployment was high, Mrs. Roosevelt joined with Miss Dickerman and Nancy Cook, her friends and political associates, in establishing the Val Kill Furniture Factory to give work to farm youths in the winter months.

Mrs. Roosevelt commuted every week between Albany and New York City, where as vice-principal of the Todhunter School she taught civics and English literature three days weekly. She is shown here at graduation.

With all her activities her interest in politics never lagged. She is seated in the background while FDR presides at a meeting of governors from various states who were seeking ways to combat the depression.

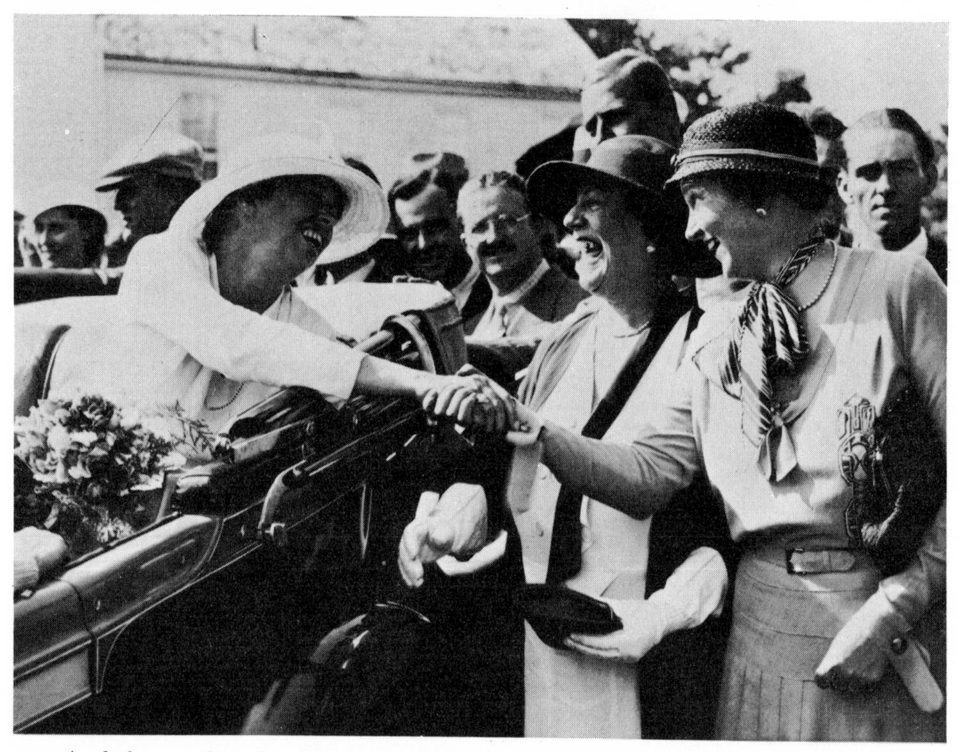

And she continued to move about and meet with different women's groups.

Entertaining Admiral Richard E. Byrd at the Governor's Mansion in Albany.

At Christmas with her husband and family she helped trim the tree before he read *A Christmas Carol*.

A holiday at Hyde Park with FDR and Missy Le Hand, his secretary, in the pool near the Val Kill Furniture factory.

Serving refreshments at a picnic.

Eleanor Roosevelt at her desk preparing campaign matter for her husband's gubernatorial race in 1930.

Mrs. Roosevelt and Louis McHenry Howe discussing plans for the future as they fly back to New York City from Warm Springs after a visit with FDR in 1932.

When FDR was nominated for the presidency in July of 1932, he wanted to save time, and dispensing with a formal notification ceremony, became the first candidate to fly to a convention to make his acceptance speech. And he took his family along with him from Albany.

Once again Eleanor Roosevelt accompanied her husband on a campaign tour.

Eleanor Roosevelt listens while her husband reads Herbert Hoover's congratulatory message on FDR's victory at the polls.

Eleanor Roosevelt, who never had lived in a home of her own, now had another house that belonged to others, but this time the owners were the people of the United States. Here she is leaving the White House on foot with "Ike" Hoover, the chief usher, after inspecting her new household.

The old order changes. . . . The wife of the new President of the United States follows Mrs. Hoover to the inauguration ceremonies.

Franklin D. Roosevelt, "a cripple who taught a crippled nation how to walk again," is sworn in as the President of the United States. The faith Eleanor Roosevelt, in the crowd at the far left, had expressed so many years ago—"I'm sure you'll really amount to something someday"—had come true.

4. The First Lady

It was a farewell party for Eleanor Roosevelt at the Women's Trade Union League in New York, just before she moved into the White House. No more would the women expect her to come to meetings with a pail of cocoa and a box of cookies, spend evenings reading and discussing things with unemployed girls, make reports on her inspection of sweatshop toilets. Somebody at the party even wrote a song kidding about her new first lady responsibilities—how she now would have to be so careful of everything she said and did and how she would have to tone down her social conscience and have a lot of tea parties.

After the song was over, Eleanor Roosevelt stood up and smiled and said firmly, "I shall be myself, as always."

It wasn't easy. Some unwritten, unspoken standard of tight tradition had silhouetted a pattern of a president's wife: preside at formal dinners, pose with prominent guests, handshake at afternoon teas, launch an occasional ship, greet the Girl Scouts, stay in the background, stay at home, stay silent.

Eleanor Roosevelt knew the pattern well. She had watched her aunt, Mrs. Theodore Roosevelt, fill it to the full—and she wanted none of it.

But the choice was not hers. She had always believed that a wife's life must adjust to her husband's career. The only alternative now was to make this adjustment in a personal pattern that no president's wife has ever duplicated, before or since.

The White House chief usher felt the first shocks:

Who ever heard of a newly elected president's wife refusing a limousine ride from her hotel to the White House, because she wanted to walk? Who ever heard of a president's wife actually moving and arranging her own furniture, operating the elevator herself, scrambling and serving eggs for her family, and filling four long legal sheets with a new highly organized outline of household schedules?

This was but the beginning. Eleanor Roosevelt soon became a constant column item, a widely repeated joke, a national headline. Always she seemed to be traveling, lecturing, writing, inspecting, teaching, interviewing, speaking her mind, demanding action, pressuring for a cause. As Gerald Johnson put it, the betting was not on whether she would ruin her husband, but on how quickly she would do it. No other woman of our time so soon earned so much love and so much hate.

And the ones who hated, circulated a question: Why didn't she stay home and take care of her own family?

It was a hard and hurtful question but it demanded answer. What could she say?

The White House was never her home. She once told somebody that she always felt when she broke a dish that she was breaking a piece of history. But it was so much more than that. Her husband was so pressured that the only time she could really talk to him was just before bedtime. And her five children were scattered all over the country, grown individuals, living their own lives, making their own mistakes.

But when they needed her, she was there. When Franklin, Jr., called her from Virginia before dawn to tell her of his auto accident, she was there two hours later holding his hands while the doctor sewed in the stitches. When James had a serious stomach operation in Minnesota, she was in the hospital hall, waiting and praying. When Anna had a baby in Seattle, she was with her all through the labor pains. When Elliott decided on a divorce, she flew to California to make sure that his decision was absolute, that the love was gone. And when John, her youngest, called from Boston late at night, worried about the birth of his first baby, she caught a midnight train and was there with a mother's comfort.

The critical questions continued: all right, even if she didn't want to stay at home, why did she do all those undignified things—go down into a coal mine, ladle out soup to unemployed, settle a strike, examine the filth of a sharecropper's camp, pay an unexpected visit to bonus marchers, tour the slums of Puerto Rico, the back alleys of Washington, the women's prisons and work camps and mental hospitals?

Why?

She went because her husband asked her to go. She was not only a president's wife; she was his other self. He needed her eyes, ears, legs, energy, conscience—he needed her truth. A prime problem of a president is to find advisers who are not awed of the office, who are not "yes men." After Louis Howe's death, Eleanor Roosevelt was one of the few the president could count on completely to report exactly what she saw, heard, felt. If she believed something strongly enough, she would disagree, argue, say no, and he couldn't kid her out of it.

Somebody said she went to the people and brought them to the president.

On her first night home from any trip anywhere she and her husband usually had dinner alone together to talk about it. The housekeeper remembered the loud private laughter of the two of them, and remarked at the pity that they couldn't have more time together because they seemed to enjoy each other so much. He called her "Ma" and laughed at the way she had ditched her secret-service agents and even learned how to shoot a gun. He had a portrait of her on his office door and once he told Frances Perkins, "That's just the way Eleanor looks, you know—lovely hair, pretty eyes. And she always looks magnificent in evening clothes, doesn't she?"

These few private dinners meant a sharing of intimacy with information. And then perhaps at the next cabinet meeting President Franklin D. Roosevelt would say: "My missus says that people are working for wages way below the minimum set by the NRA in the town she visited last week," or "My missus says that people are leaving the Dust Bowl in droves because they haven't any chance there." FDR's secretary, Grace Tully, said, "It was not unusual to hear him predicate an entire line of reasoning upon a statement that, 'My missus told me so and so. . . .' "

This missus once had written: "A man or woman in public life . . . must keep an open mind, but when they have listened and know what they think themselves, they must have the courage to stand by that."

When her husband mentioned at dinner that he planned to promote a certain diplomat, she interrupted, "But, Franklin, you know he's simply dreadful." And when her husband asked her to document this, she had her evidence on his desk the next morning.

When the Daughters of the American Revolution refused to

permit Marian Anderson to sing at Constitution Hall because of her skin color, Eleanor Roosevelt resigned from the D.A.R. and invited Miss Anderson to sing in the White House.

When she felt that qualified women were being sidetracked from government and politics, she personally helped organize the Women's Division of the Democratic party, got women put on the party's platform committee for the first time, made five campaign speeches in the congressional campaign for Caroline O'Day, and even sent memos to her husband: "The feeling is that this is a committee on which a woman or women could well have been appointed."

When Pearl Harbor provoked a hysterical hate of everything Japanese, she spent the very next day in Seattle, getting herself photographed with a group of Nisei, pleading in the press that these American citizens of Japanese descent be treated as friends and neighbors and the loyal Americans that they were.

It took courage.

Some of her courage seemed more like simple stubbornness. The harder the press pounded on the make-up and purpose of the American Youth Congress, the more closely she identified herself with it, the longer she took to admit—even to herself—that the gradual infiltration of Communists had made the organization valueless.

Her habit of picking and promoting protégés—usually young people—became a particular target of national mocking. She only heightened the publicity by posing for photographs with young dancers demonstrating "The Eleanor Glide."

If this was a loud laugh—and it was—she defended her young friends sharply, even against her children. When one of her sons criticized the manners of some of her young friends, she told him off: "And who are you to talk of their bad manners?" she said.

"You were brought up in plenty. You never had to fight for an education, you never had to look for a job. Who are you to talk of young people who have had to fight for everything they got, and didn't get much?"

Nobody fought harder than she did for the people who couldn't fight for themselves. Sometimes it meant visiting a local official to see what could be done about a large family facing eviction and sometimes it meant getting her husband to write "a very strong letter" to a governor about a Negro she felt was being railroaded for a crime he didn't commit.

It meant taking the wives of congressmen on a tour of slum alleys within sight of the Capitol, so they could tell their husbands about the shame of what they saw. She kept at it until Congress appropriated money for a housing project. She stayed with it from the demolition to the construction, even checking to make sure that all the families had been properly relocated.

It meant acting as White House instigator to sell her husband on the National Youth Administration, which gave thousands of young people skilled training during the depression—and then constantly spot-checking these projects for abuses or possible improvements. She did the same thing with the Federal Theater and Federal Writers projects.

It meant making unannounced visits everywhere so that she would see actual conditions instead of polished showcases. As a result, she forced Congress to clean up the pesthouse condition of a Washington mental hospital, upgrade school-lunch programs, overhaul the Children's Receiving Home.

It meant a White House garden party for some sixty girls from the National Training School—all of them from sixteen to twenty-two, black and white, all convicted at least three times as shoplifters, prostitutes, or vagrants. It was a way of pinpointing national attention on their miserable place of detention, and it worked—the school got badly needed improvements.

It meant testifying before a congressional committee on the sickening sight of sharecropper camps until Congress agreed to appropriate five million dollars for new camps.

It meant a White House lunch with NRA boss General Hugh Johnson and Secretary of Labor Frances Perkins that resulted in a ruling of equal pay for women in NRA codes.

It meant a broadside at Congress when they first thought of cutting relief appropriations. "I wish these congressmen would answer some of the questions which come to me," she said. Then she read from some of the pitiful letters of poverty which flooded into her regularly.

Then she told the story—something she herself saw—of a skinny girl in a West Virginia shanty town of unemployed coal miners. The girl was chasing her little brother who was hugging a scrawny pet rabbit, and the girl said, "He doesn't think we'll eat it, but we will." That was the same area where people lived in worn tents and the Christmas surprise for kids was a carrot.

Eleanor Roosevelt took whole parties of press and government officials to see the area until she saw new factories, new houses, new human beings. One of the developments even called itself, "Eleanor Unincorporated."

Congress changed its mind for a while.

And yet, with all this, one critic felt perfectly qualified to call her "a diarist and a dilettante."

She *was* a diarist. "My Day" faithfully reported what happened to her—perhaps without much sophistication or sparkle or humor. One group of forty wrote their newspaper, "Of all the nonsensical and demented nonsense, it takes the bun." But it appeared in hundreds of newspapers, Republican included, and it sometimes served as an important trial balloon for some of FDR's ideas. More than once he was overheard telling her, "Darling, you can't use this for your column—it's off the record."

Her mail kept piling up—more than three hundred thousand letters received that first year in the White House—and she selected the most important ones for her husband's night table.

Her lecture tour—some twenty-five thousand miles a year—served as still another source for FDR, a firsthand report on the sharpest questions of the public mind.

But perhaps her greatest fun—and the best trial balloon for FDR—was her press conference, in which she discussed every political issue, however hot: everything from the anti-lynching bill to the Supreme Court controversy and Soviet Russia's invasion of Poland.

Being a trial balloon made her a more obvious target for criticism, and some of it included vicious gutter stuff. It seemed to bother her husband much more than it bothered her, because he probably realized how much of it was his fault. One visitor vividly remembers being with FDR, listening to some commentator who suddenly switched to an attack on Mrs. Roosevelt, and how quickly FDR turned it off, his face pained.

But if some hated, many loved. Heywood Broun reported in his column that the pecan workers of San Antonio wanted her to run for president, and added that it wasn't such a bad idea because "It seems to me at the moment that Eleanor Roosevelt has a deeper and closer understanding of the needs and aspirations of millions of Americans than any other person in public life."

Somebody else put it another way. It was after the 1932 election, and the phrase was, "Now we have a pair of presidents."

It was partly true.

She was a Roosevelt before she married a Roosevelt. She was a president's niece before she was a president's wife. She knew well the First Lady's expected pattern, the tight tradition: stay in the background, stay at home, stay silent. She wanted none of that, and yet here she was, despite herself, alone at her husband's Inaugural Ball, caught by the excitement of it. "I didn't dare go to bed nights lest something interesting happen while I was asleep," she told a friend. "We were all up all hours. Finally Friday night, things seemed to have quieted down pretty much and we all went to bed fairly early. At 12:30, however, I was awakened by the telephone in my room and told about the Los Angeles earthquake. I went in and wakened my husband and told him about it. He told me to wake up Mr. Howe and Mr. Early, two of his secretaries, and to get in touch with Los Angeles at once.

"But they say the wires are all down," I told him.

"Well, get in touch with Los Angeles anyway," he said.

After finishing the story then, she confided to her friend, "You can get a thrill out of history in the making, even if you are only an onlooker. . . ." She would soon be much more than an onlooker.

Relaxing in his office, FDR looked for a long time at the portrait of his wife, then suddenly said to his visitor, "Eleanor always looks magnificent in evening clothes, doesn't she?"

"THE ONLY THING WE HAVE TO FEAR . . .

. . . IS FEAR ITSELF."

The blood and national shame of the first bonus march riots came back fresh when the second bonus marchers now came to Washington. Louis Howe saw them on behalf of the President and promised help. "Louis was so sick, he couldn't walk," remembered Mrs. Roosevelt, "but he insisted I drive him down to their camp, then told me, 'You're going in there and you're going to see everything about that camp. You're not going to miss a thing.' And I went, and I saw everything they could show me of their miserable quarters, then came back to Louis and answered all his questions. And Louis did help them get money."

At a farewell party for her at the Women's Trade Union League, somebody kiddingly said she would now have to tone down her social conscience, and she answered, "I shall be myself, as always."

After she finished speaking to the crowd at the government camp, the chairman asked for questions, and some heckler commented, "Watch her wilt." But she didn't. Some of the questions were daggered and digging, with malice aforethought, because these were not the happiest of people. Still, she answered them all, simply, pleasantly, honestly in her same precise, hyperenunciated manner. When it was all over, the same heckler told a newspaperwoman, "Well, at least she doesn't talk about the poor as if they were numbers."

Some newspapers wondered aloud why she poked her nose in so many places, why she didn't stay home. Her answer was simple (though she never said it): she went because her husband wanted her to go, see, ask questions, find out, and then come back and tell him the truth. She went because he couldn't.

"Either we are going to share, or have nothing," she once told a group of Junior Leaguers. Whether it was the smelly slums of Puerto Rico or the back alleys of Washington, she pressured her husband and Congress until she got something done. In Puerto Rico they named their first housing project "Eleanor Roosevelt."

"You know, my missus gets around a lot," FDR told his cabinet meeting. Or, "My missus says they have typhoid in that district." Or, "My missus says the people are leaving the Dust Bowl in droves because they haven't any chance there."

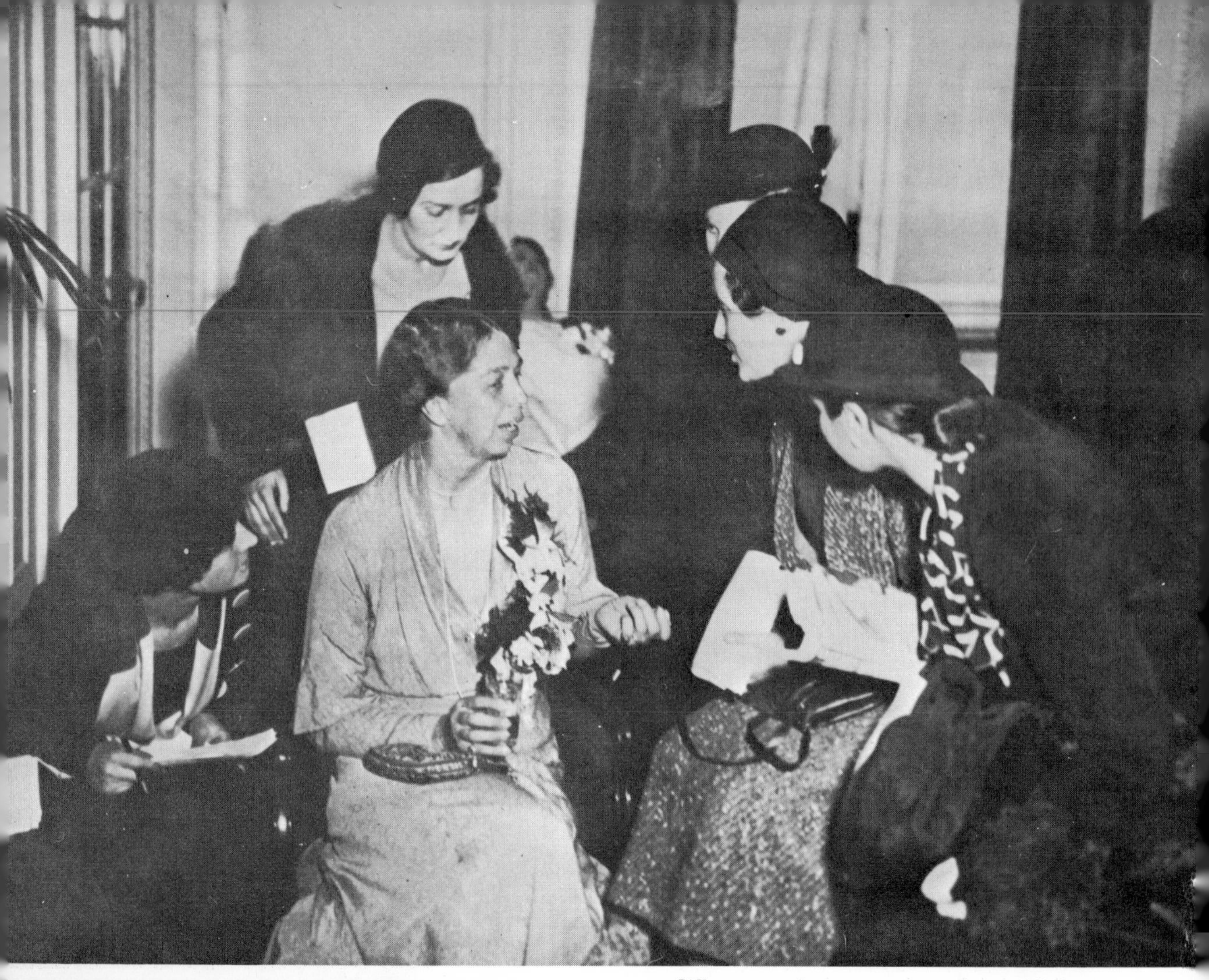

Whenever she saw wrong, she publicized it, and her regular Monday morning press conference made news—sometimes more news than her husband might like. Still, it often served his purpose, as a trial balloon for his new ideas, even though it increased criticism of her.

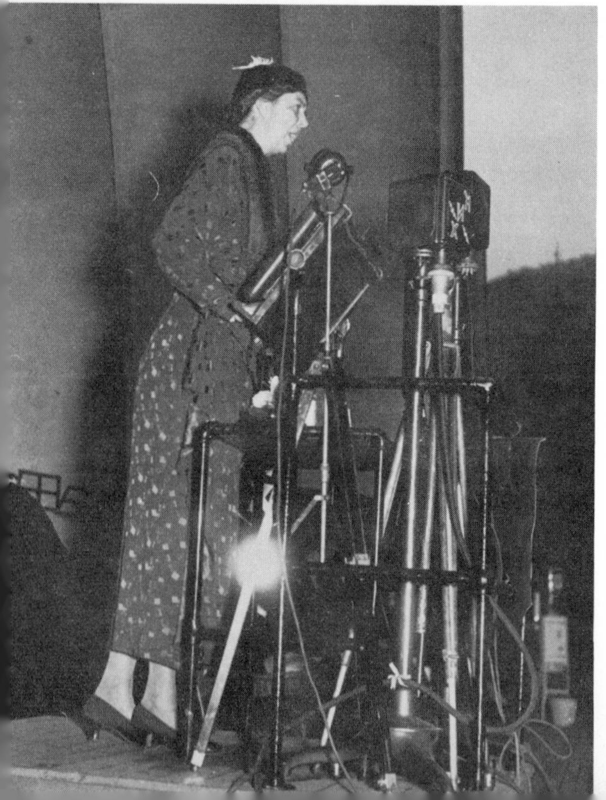

She always talked without notes, some sixty-eight speeches that first year, and the high giggle had long gone from her voice. Plus that, she had a weekly radio program that paid her about $500 a minute. One of her listeners complained that he didn't know anyone who was worth that much, and she quickly agreed. What she didn't say was that all her earned income—some $75,000 that first year—went to charity and "not one penny was put away for herself."

When she felt that qualified women were being sidetracked from government and politics, she personally helped organize the Women's Division of the Democratic party.

"Just for one day, God, PLEASE make her *tired. . . .*" That was the highly publicized prayer of the weary newspaperwomen who tried to trail after her—some 40,000 miles that first year. Other things they reported: Eleanor never felt exhausted, knitted to rest her eyes, was up for breakfast at 8:30 no matter when she went to sleep, didn't take naps in the afternoon, always read herself to sleep but never suffered insomnia, had her hair done once a week but never had a facial because she never had time—although she would have loved one!

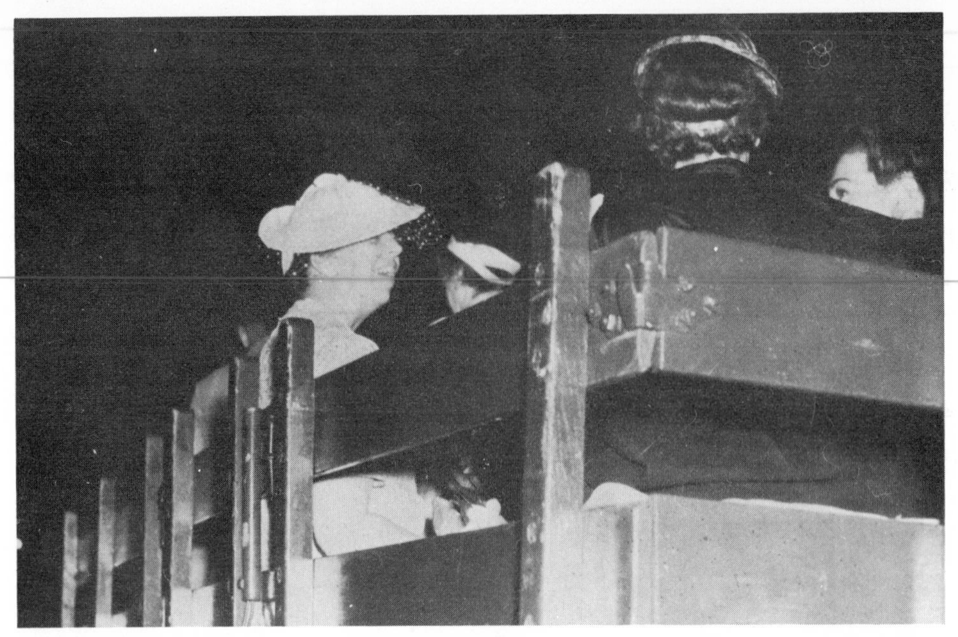

"You know, one of the great things about Eleanor," her husband said, "is that she's already thrown off the Secret Service. They can't keep up with her. The result is that she goes where she wants to, talks to everybody, and does she learn something!" Whatever she learned, she put in a private post office—a basket on her husband's night table.

Her own five children were scattered, and she had to travel to see them, but whenever they needed her, she was there: a new baby, sickness, an operation, a divorce, an auto accident, and here a point of pride. She is at the Groton School in Massachusetts watching her son Franklin, Jr., stroke his crew to victory.

If it had been a long trip—a three months' inspection tour of government agencies or a report on the Carribean—her first meal at home was always alone with her husband so that she could tell him everything freshly and fully as she saw it and felt it.

Typical of her reporting trips was a tour of the Norris Dam in Tennessee, a $34,000,000 power project that FDR wanted to know more about. Finding facts included a cable-car ride 400 feet above the Clinch River. Always, she tried to combine her lecture tour with side-trip inspections.

"For gosh sakes, here comes Mrs. Roosevelt!"

Drawing by Robt. Day. © 1933 The New Yorker Magazine, Inc.

She laughed at this just as she laughed at the national joke that Admiral Byrd set two places for supper in his South Pole shack "just in case Eleanor should drop in."

A *New York Times* reporter insists that it was the cartoon that gave her the idea of actually going down into a coal mine. But when she saw the dark, dank, working conditions and the pitiful poverty of the miners, it was no longer funny.

Back at the White House, the receiving lines never seemed to stop. She learned some trade tricks: "Don't let the line stop, keep it gently moving along; grasp the fingers of the handshaker firmly, never permitting him to get a firm grip on your hand; gently draw him past as you say, 'How do you do? I'm so glad to see you'; stop about every thousand handshakes to get a drink of water; bend you knees just a little, and frequently—nobody will notice."

She once told a convention of the Daughters of the American Revolution that while it was important to be willing to die for your country, it was even more important to prepare yourselves to live for it. She said this in Washington's Constitution Hall. Later, when the DAR refused to permit Marion Anderson to sing in that hall because of her skin color, Eleanor Roosevelt resigned from the DAR.

One of the first things she did in the White House was to cut the social calendar to a crisp—mostly because she felt it was out of tune with the depression. But one thing she would never cut was the Easter Egg Hunt on the White House lawn for the thousands of children from everywhere. Somebody said of her: "Of course she loves children, she had so many of them." And they are all over the world.

Once she wrote a parody:

"The world is so full of a number of things
I find myself watching all three rings,
Wondering if our circus wild
Will meet the needs of next year's child."

Here she is at another circus with her granddaughter, Sistie Dall.

Teaching at Todhunter was one of the things she loved most—and she even had granddaughter Sistie there. One of the courses she taught was called "Happenings," and part of the course involved a weekend in the White House for some students. One student remembered the time she daringly wandered out of her White House bedroom, went into the President's study with another giggly friend, then sat in the President's chair until she heard his approaching wheel chair, and just managed to sidle behind a screen and sneak out of the room when he entered. "And I never told Mrs. Roosevelt."

Another school she concerned herself with was Arthurdale High School in West Virginia. This was a pitiful community of unemployed coal miners living in shacks on raw carrots until she publicized their plight, badgered government officials and wealthy friends to put up factories, homes. She was there to hand out diplomas to the first high-school graduates, and here she is dancing with one of them.

A reporter once asked her if it was true that she bought four hats in two minutes. She smiled, shook her head, and assured the reporter that it was a slight exaggeration. Actually, she said, it took her about six minutes. Another woman reporter wanted to know what she planned to wear at an upcoming diplomatic reception. "I haven't the slightest idea," she said, "but I might as well decide right now. That cream satin. You remember it."

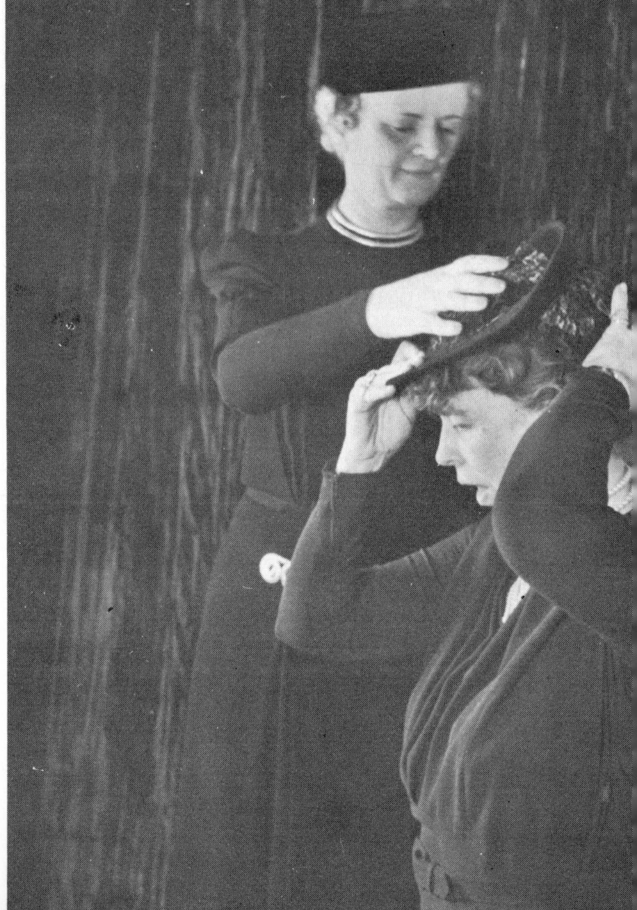

Christening, like handshaking, meant mastering a special technique, a twist of the wrist, a certain amount of aim, and a strong arm—and another dress at the cleaners. She soon created some kind of christening record—everything from superliners to the first Pan American Clipper to fly the Pacific to a small boy's rowboat in Campobello.

Her days grew so packed and timetabled that she discovered that the only time available for horseback riding was before breakfast. But even then the public eye watched, and when her horse Dot dropped her in a mudhole, it meant another headline. She then told the press, "I fell off very gracefully, and Washington may just as well get used to it because I do it regularly."

Sara Delano Roosevelt at the Metropolitan Art Museum.

Eleanor Roosevelt at the Gridiron Widows' party.

Her first recorded victory over government red tape was her insistence that horrified park officials put a swing on the White House lawn for her grandchildren. "I have lived all my life where there were swings on old trees and I never saw one harmed," she said.

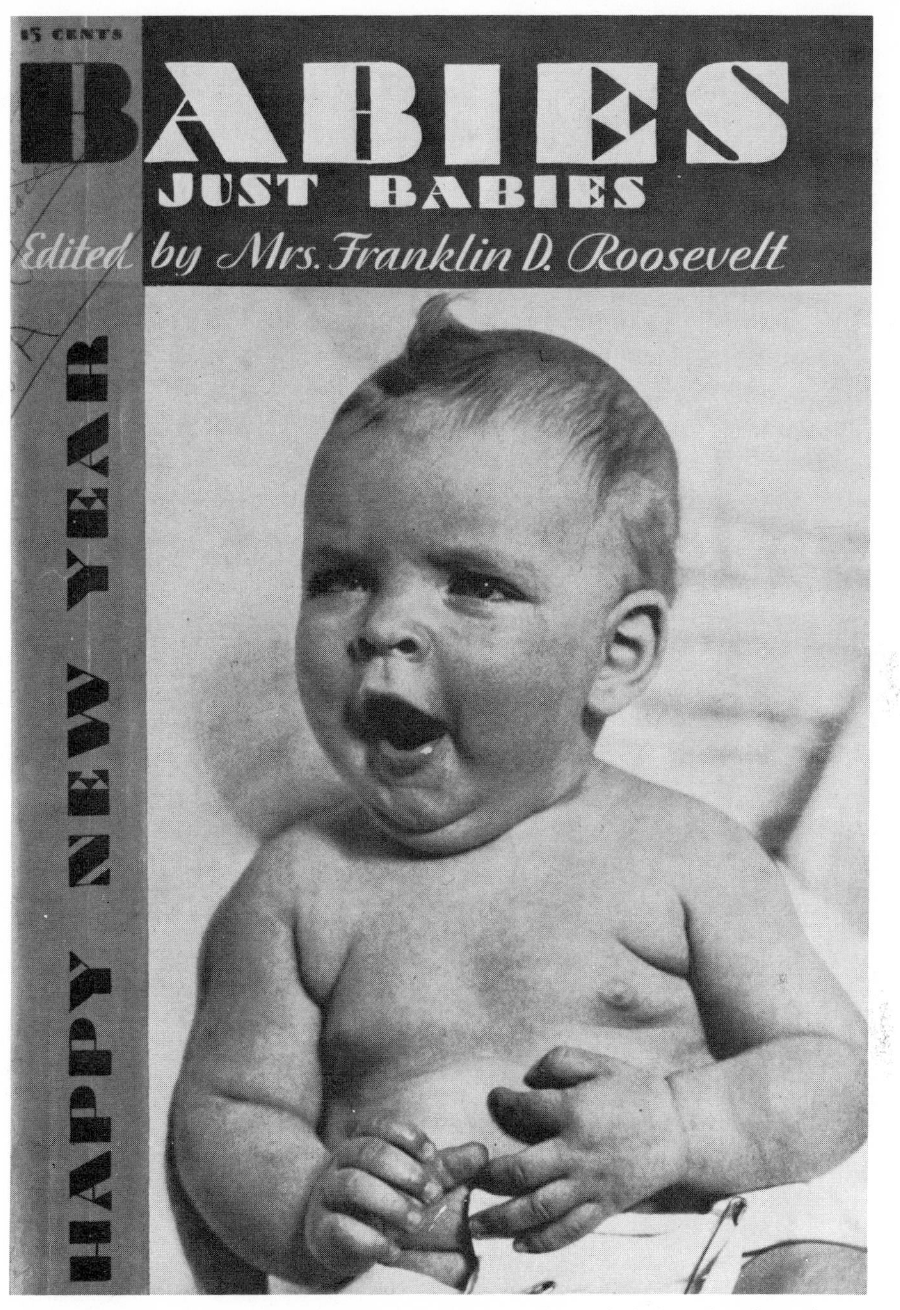

Not only did she edit this magazine for a short time, with her daughter Anna, but she had also edited the *Women's Democratic News* and wrote all kinds of books, such as *A Trip to Washington with Bobby and Betty*, *Democracy and Religion*, and *It's Up to the Women*—in which she said that if women wanted to combine homes and careers, they should do it. Or at least, try.

My Day By Eleanor Roosevelt

THE WHITE HOUSE, Washington, Dec. 30.—I wonder if anyone else glories in cold and snow without, an open fire within, and the luxury of a tray of food all by one's self in one's room. I realize that it sounds extremely selfish and a little odd to look upon such an occasion as festive. Nevertheless, Saturday night was a festive occasion, for I spent it that way.

The house was full of young people, my husband had a cold and was in bed with milk toast for his supper, so I said a polite goodnight to everyone at 7:30, closed my door, lit my fire and settled down to a nice long evening by myself. I read things which I had in my briefcase for weeks—a report on educational work in the CCC camps, a copy of Progressive Education dealing with the problems of youth, the first copy of a magazine edited by a group of young people, a chapter in manuscript, and I went to sleep at 10:30. Because I haven't been to bed for weeks before 1 A. M. and often later, this was so unusual that I work this morning with a feeling that I must have slept for several years.

Yesterday was a grand contrast, with sixteen for lunch. My guest on my right was Mr. Regan, of Groton School, who long watched over our boys and the boys of many other people and who is, I think, one of the best beloved masters in the school. He certainly is a very wise man and has a delicious sense of humor.

One youngster who is staying with us here remarked:—

"Every meal is different in this house. Yesterday we talked about philosophies of government. Today we talked about movies and punging." I smiled to myself, for it would be very hard to be dull with only two people over 30 at the table, all the others bursting with youth and energy.

One reader described her column: "Of all the nonsensical and demented nonsense, it takes the bun." But among other things, it was an excellent sounding board for many FDR ideas in some 180 newspapers, many of them Republican.

He called her "Babs," and she called him "Franklin." She only called him "the President" when she wanted to tease him.

Aside from shaking hands, pouring tea, and catching planes, another Eleanor Roosevelt record is that she has passed out probably more hot dogs to more people at more picnics than most of the women of the world.

She was always a poor sailor, but her husband and sons were born to it. This 1933 trip was FDR's first return to Campobello since his polio attack. They called this ship the *Amberjack*.

These two women shared this man only in the beginning. By the time of this picture, the mother had stepped back, and the wife had emerged as a mute voice suddenly made articulate, a full partner—without any reservations.

Early Christmas morning—every Christmas—she would wake before everybody else, close her husband's bedroom window, start the fire in the fireplace, then crawl back into her bedroom, waiting for the squealing sounds of grandchildren.

Her political campaign role with her husband had been fixed in 1932 and stayed that way. She served as a showcase: wave from the train's rear platform, smile, shake hands, accept flowers, and walk the dog at the siding whenever the train stops. No political speeches. But she could speak, and did, when her friend Caroline O'Day ran for Congress. And she could, and did, help lay the detailed groundwork for the Women's Division of the Democratic Party.

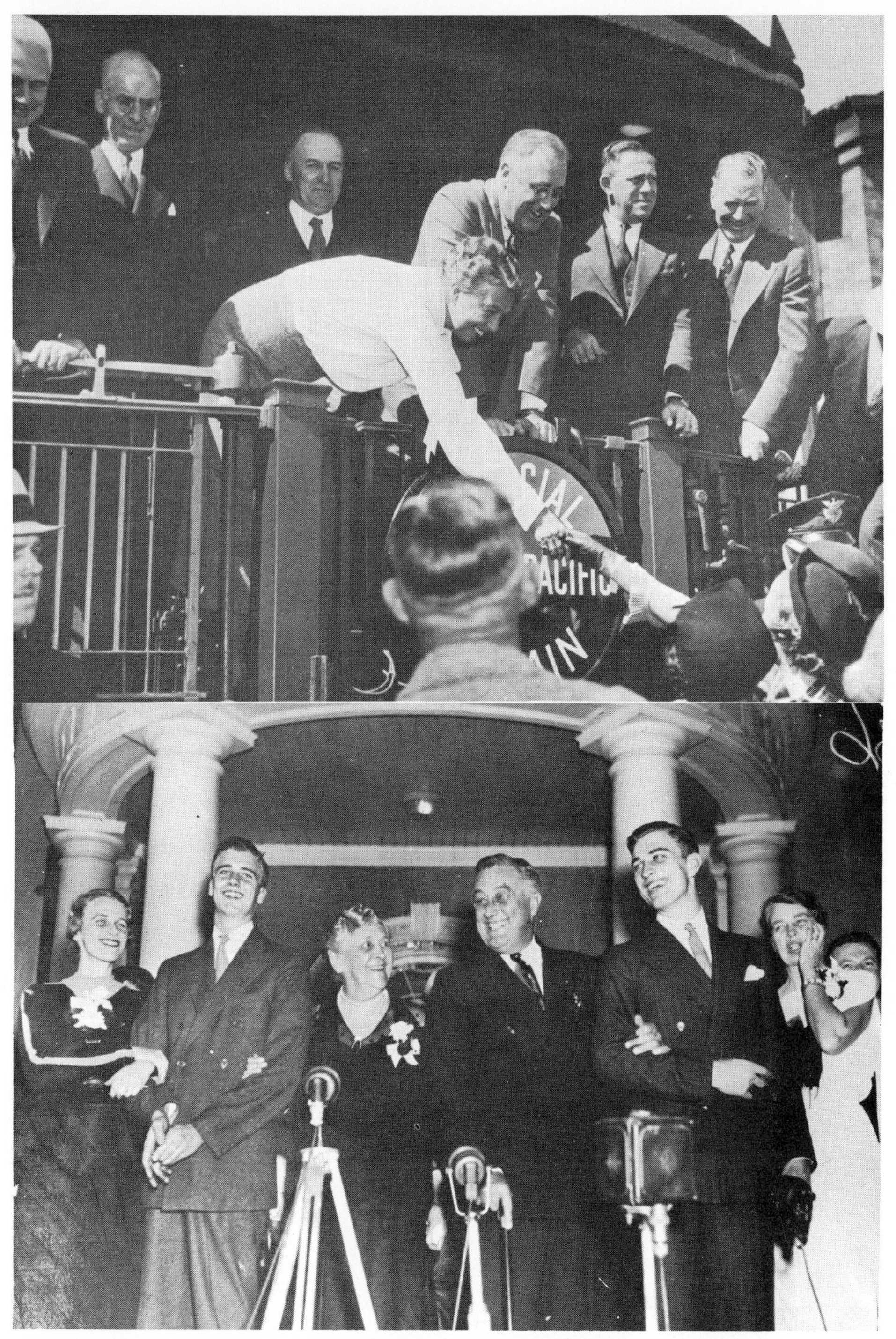

Even on the campaign train, she was one of the few who could argue and disagree with her husband on issues and people. She had written such a detailed analysis of the upcoming 1936 campaign that National Chairman James Farley wrote a twenty-page letter to answer it. Farley called her "the most practical woman I ever met in politics." Certainly, at their Hyde Park celebration, part of the victory was hers.

5. The War Years

Every year the Women's National Press Club had a Gridiron Widow's dinner and their obvious lampooning target was Eleanor Roosevelt. Several times she saw herself going to Mars, visiting Admiral Byrd in the South Pole, sitting as the newest member of the United States Supreme Court—knitting during arguments and publishing the court's decision in advance in her newspaper column. Once they featured jingles about her, one of them called "Eleanor St. Vitus My Day" which went:

Hi diddle diddle, the cat and the fiddle,
The cow jumped over the moon,
The moon laughed and laughed and said, "You're too late
Eleanor passed here at noon."

Still another time a skit showed a frazzled inmate of the "Eleanor Roosevelt Home for Exhausted Newspaper Women" clasping her hands and praying, "Dear God, let me pray the prayer they say that Franklin prays. Just for one day, God, PLEASE make her *tired*! Dear God, just for ONE DAY!"

Even back in the White House her housekeeper said that she always moved at a dogtrot, so fast that she actually bent forward. On a typical day she still managed a horseback ride before breakfast, some midmorning meetings with government officials, a mail session dictating thirty letters at a clip interrupted by phone calls, a press conference, a luncheon with the highly aristocratic Monday Sewing Class of New York City, a tour of the White House for some visiting New England fishermen who afterward commented, "She ain't stuck up, she ain't dressed up and she ain't afeard to talk." Then there was a tea for a French journalist, joining FDR to greet the French premier, a tea for the Canadian prime minister, and another for a miscellaneous group of ladies and their children, and finally a family dinner.

Sometime in between all this she worried with the housekeeper on how to cut costs, replace the rickety kitchen, double the order on doilies, get the curtains turned, the tablecloths darned, the worn rugs rewoven. She also had to deal with some private memos from her husband:

> Do you remember that about a month ago I got sick of chicken because I got it (between lunch and dinner) at least six times a week? The chicken situation has definitely improved, but "they" have substituted sweetbreads, and for the past month I have been getting sweetbreads about six times a week.
>
> I am getting to the point where my stomach positively rebels and this does not help my relations with foreign powers. I bit two of them today.

And there were still other wifely duties such as firmly reminding her husband that he needed a new formal suit because his trousers were showing signs of wear. And when he moaned, she added that she was going to call in the tailor and have one made.

One of her mother-in-law's tricks that she adopted was to invite people for dinner who had something to say that she felt he ought to hear—even if he didn't want to. John Gunther tells of the time that FDR loudly complained to his wife that he didn't want to see some student she was interested in because "I want dinner to be a relaxation, not an excuse for business." Nearby, one of their guests, Aubrey Williams, burst out laughing, and FDR wanted to know why. Williams explained that Mrs. Roosevelt had invited him to dinner that night to tell FDR about his project. FDR joined in the laughter, then listened carefully.

But Mrs. Roosevelt didn't always win. Leon Henderson witnessed the time when she plainly rebuked the President while he was there. "You and I, Mr. Henderson," she said, "were morally right, but too weak." Then she looked right at FDR, and continued talking to Henderson, "We should have pushed him harder." FDR stayed silent.

Those who were there vividly remember another time when she "raised unshirted hell" about the stupidity of the plowing-under program of pigs and cotton when millions were hungry and ragged. Often, however, FDR would goad her into an argument on some policy question, and then the next day amaze her at lunch by advocating exactly what she had said.

A friend described her defense of her projects as "passionate," and Mrs. Roosevelt answered, "I hardly think the word 'passionate' applies to me." The passion is there but it's buried deep, almost completely controlled. After she came to the White House, nobody ever saw tears in her eyes, and there were times that called for tears. "I have learned to feel one way inside at such times and outwardly to go on like an automaton . . . but it takes all the discipline I have acquired in life to keep on talking and smiling and to concentrate on the conversation."

This is a family of stoics who can control their emotions even with each other, but the emotion is still there, the warmth real, the bond tight. After a meeting at a Murray Hill hotel in New

York in 1938, a woman stood up to ask, "Mrs. Roosevelt, isn't it true that the President's illness has affected his mind?"

The room hushed as she answered, and the words came, stripped and simple, "Yes, I think it has," she said. "I think it has made him more sensitive to the feelings of people."

This was part of the price she paid, and sometimes the price seemed too high. But sometimes it was fun. She had fun making her own plans for the arrival of the King and Queen of England—and some of her plans put the State Department protocol people in a small panic.

She felt this: formal dinners are fine and dandy, and fancy foods are all right, but the King and Queen had come to America to see and feel and taste America. That's why her meals for them featured everything American—from potato chips to corn pone. And that's why she invited such entertainers as Kate Smith, an Indian princess, and the Coon Creek Girls from Pinchem-Tight Hollow in the Renfro Valley of Kentucky. That's why she organized a New Deal tea for the royal family so they could meet government officials who dealt with the American problems of housing and health and labor and people. And that's why she overruled her mother-in-law and insisted on having an informal picnic for the royalty up at Hyde Park—featuring hot dogs.

When she and her husband stood at Hyde Park railroad station and sang an Auld Lang Syne good-by, with their neighbors, to the King and Queen, she felt a sudden sadness, because the edge of war was coming closer to England, and to us. She was a mother of four sons, and she wanted no war. Her first talk as first lady was to call on America's youth to make future wars impossible. When she saw a movie of a bombing in Spain, she wrote:

"I felt positively disgusted with human beings. How can we be such fools as to go on senselessly taking human life in this way? Why the women in every nation do not rise up and refuse to bring children into a world of this kind is beyond my understanding."

But the growing aggression of Germany and Italy deepened her understanding. And one morning at five o'clock the troubled voice of her husband came over the telephone to wake and tell her that the Nazis had invaded Poland. So when a young man at a meeting belligerently told her, "Tell Franklin the Yanks aren't coming," she silenced him by saying, "Listen, my child, what happens if the Nazis come here?"

Diplomacy often tied FDR's tongue, but his wife had no qualms, and her condemnation of aggression was loud and clear. It drew much backfire, including a front-page editorial from Premier Mussolini's *Popolo d'Italia* suggesting that an embargo on Mrs. Roosevelt would be an excellent precautionary measure if the United States wanted to keep out of war.

Fear was the most important fact of international politics, and tradition became the big issue of domestic politics—the third term. She didn't want FDR to take it. In a note to her husband two years before, referring to a friend's request for an FDR speech, Eleanor Roosevelt wrote: "She wants you for a third term and I thought this most unwise. You know, I do *not* believe in it." She kept urging him to pick a successor, even went ahead and rented a New York apartment for the two of them after election. He gave her the full impression that he would retire.

The war threat changed his mind and he carefully engineered his third-term draft. With party chairman James Farley opposed, FDR picked Harry Hopkins as his unofficial floor manager. This almost tore the convention apart and Frances Perkins got on the phone to warn of trouble.

To save her some of the mudslinging, FDR had kept his wife out of actual campaigning for him in 1932 and 1936. She had traveled with him, smiled with him, shaken hands and accepted flowers, and walked Fala along the tracks whenever the train stopped. Her main work was behind the scenes, organizing and planning the work of the Women's Division of the party. And for the 1936 campaign she did such an excellent analysis of the work to be done—in the way Louis Howe had taught her—that it took a twenty-page letter from James Farley to answer all her important questions. James Farley once said that, "Eleanor Roosevelt is the most practical woman I ever met in politics."

FDR disagreed. He always told her that she was too impatient to be a good politician, that she wanted to see results much too quickly, that she had no real sense of political timing. He changed his mind in 1940. He needed his wife badly—and as a politician. He needed her so badly that he backtracked on a promise he had made to her—that she would not have to go out to the convention in Chicago. When Perkins pointed out the convention's resentful mood because of the Hopkins-Farley split, FDR agreed that only his wife might heal the breach.

Maybe her political timing was bad, but her political sense wasn't: she refused to come unless Farley invited her, unless Farley alone met her at the plane.

The convention was a madhouse until she got up to speak, and suddenly there was a complete silence of respect from the thirty thousand while she talked—without a prepared speech, without even notes. It wasn't a great speech but it was so simple and so shrewd that it transformed a mob of delegates into a political unit.

After it was all over, congratulations came from everywhere, but it was not the biggest thing on her mind. When she spotted her friend Lorena Hickok, she called out:

"Hick, they let me fly the plane!"

En route home again the plane taxied halfway down the runway at Chicago when it was desperately waved to a stop. The White House was on the phone. Her husband wanted to tell her how pleased he was with her.

The war threat tightened the family, made Christmas more precious. As always, on Christmas Day she crept out of bed to light the fire in her husband's room and close the windows and sneak back to bed waiting for the grandchildren to come running through the corridors. Then there was her Christmas closet, which she had spent all year filling, all presents carefully indexed so nobody would get the same present twice. And her husband, again re-elected, again shoving aside the worry of war to read *A Christmas Carol* to the children.

Her wish to do something, anything at all to help in this time of trouble, pulled her into the Office of Civilian Defense to work with Mayor Fiorello La Guardia. She worked at her usual pace, sometimes not sleeping at all, refusing both salary and expenses, but it was still a mistake. She was too easy a target for everybody who hated Roosevelt, and when she felt this was hurting the OCD, she quit.

Now the war was on, and our troops were already in England waiting. FDR suggested she serve as his legs again, and visit them. Off she went with one evening dress, two day dresses, one suit, a few blouses, one pair of day shoes, and one pair of evening shoes, tagged with the code name, "Rover."

Rover filled up her notebooks with names and telephone numbers of mothers to call, talked and ate and sang with the soldiers, visited the three war orphans she had adopted, laid down the law that there would be no dress parades because she knew how soldiers hated to wait for hours just so somebody could look at them for a few minutes. And all over England she walked through miles and miles of hospital corridors.

There was that time when a fat colonel, puffing behind her, finally interrupted, "Mrs. Roosevelt, we have spent much more time here than we were supposed to. We're supposed to meet the general and the lord mayor for lunch and we're late already."

Mrs. Roosevelt simply smiled and said, "There's only one more ward, Colonel."

There was the time when Corporal Vincent Strianse of Brooklyn said, half-aloud, "Ain't she a honey!"

There was also the time when a few people wrote her, "I hope all your sons get killed."

Her four sons were all soon in combat action on the different war fronts and their letters were like all letters of sons to mothers, writing about socks received and packages en route and family gossip, all addressed to "Dearest Mummy," and one of them saying, "Mummy, I hope you don't have to do too much this summer and can get some rest at Hyde Park." Her husband had written her earlier, "Dear Babs . . . do get some real rest even if some of the mail gets 'acknowledged' instead of answered."

A long time before he had written his "dearest Babs," "The Lord only knows when this will catch up with my will-o'-the-wisp wife." But he knew the importance of her trips, and soon sent her out again, this time to the Pacific in a Red Cross uniform. She wouldn't go until he agreed to let her visit Guadalcanal, where the war was. After she left, FDR sent Admiral Halsey a secret cable asking him not to permit his wife to go to Guadalcanal.

She traveled alone then, painfully slow at typing her own column but never missing a deadline, never missing a hospital bed, and always feeling grateful that she knew America so well that she could light up so many soldiers' faces by saying simply, "I know your town." Some officers admitted that they had resented her upcoming visit but changed their minds. And Admiral Halsey was so pleased by reports that he permitted her to go to Guadalcanal.

She was no pinup and couldn't sing well ("When I was a little girl I always wanted to be able to sing and have a beautiful voice which would move people"), but she did have some special stories for the men. There was one story about the cook who pleaded for the chance to go into combat for just one day so he could kill an enemy soldier, and they finally let him go. At the day's end he returned, terribly depressed. Yes, finally toward evening he had seen an enemy soldier, but he couldn't kill him.

"Why not?" everybody wanted to know.

"Well, this guy stood up and yelled, 'To hell with Franklin D. Roosevelt,' and I just couldn't shoot a fellow Republican."

She returned home thirty pounds lighter, with even more telephone numbers to call: "I saw your son and he told me to call you." Her husband had once before written of a trip, "Everywhere I hear of the good you have done," and soon he had still another trip: the thirteen thousand miles of the Caribbean.

Her sons had warned her to keep closer to the enlisted men, and she made it a habit of getting on their breakfast chow line every morning before six, and she went to outposts and islands where women had never been before.

Back home again the fourth-term question had come up, and she was hoping hard FDR would say no because she knew the measure of his tiredness. He would no longer react the same way when she argued with him about something, and so she stopped arguing. Instead of important letters on his night table, she now put funny ones: somebody's suggestion that we collect hives of hornets, bees, and wasps, put them in planes, and drop them on enemy lines to create confusion.

She campaigned with him, sat in the open-car ride through New York in the rain, watched the election victory without pleasure. She wanted to go to Yalta with him, but he said no, and later took Anna, his daughter.

And then one day he was down in Warm Springs and she was at a benefit party in Washington when the call came. It was a simple message for her to come to the White House, but she somehow knew. She still automatically said good-by to her hostess, then sat in the car with her hands clenched, storing up strength for a blow of fate. When it came, she was ready. The tears were all inside. At Warm Springs the photographers waited respectfully without their cameras, and she went inside the room and closed the door, alone with the body of her husband.

Of him she had said: "He might have been happier with a wife who was completely uncritical. That I was never able to be, and he had to find it in other people. Nevertheless, I think I sometimes acted as a spur, even though the spurring was not always wanted or welcome. I was one of those who served his purpose."

Now she would serve her own.

This was her second ride in a presidential parade, but this time she sat beside her husband. Just before the first ride, four years before, an admirer had said, "Now we'll have a pair of presidents." And one of her critics had said, "Sure I like something about her—her husband."

If she felt full of personal questions the first time, she now knew how much stretch there was in her future pattern of living, and she now knew the strength of their partnership. Noted country editor William Allen White, of the *Emporia Gazette* in Kansas, who spent his editorial votes for Republicans, told her, "My dear, I don't care if he runs for a third or fourth term as long as he lets you run the bases, keep the score, and win the game."

They waited in the pouring rain to hear his words about ". . . one third of a nation . . ."

". . . ill clothed . . ."

". . . ill housed . . ."

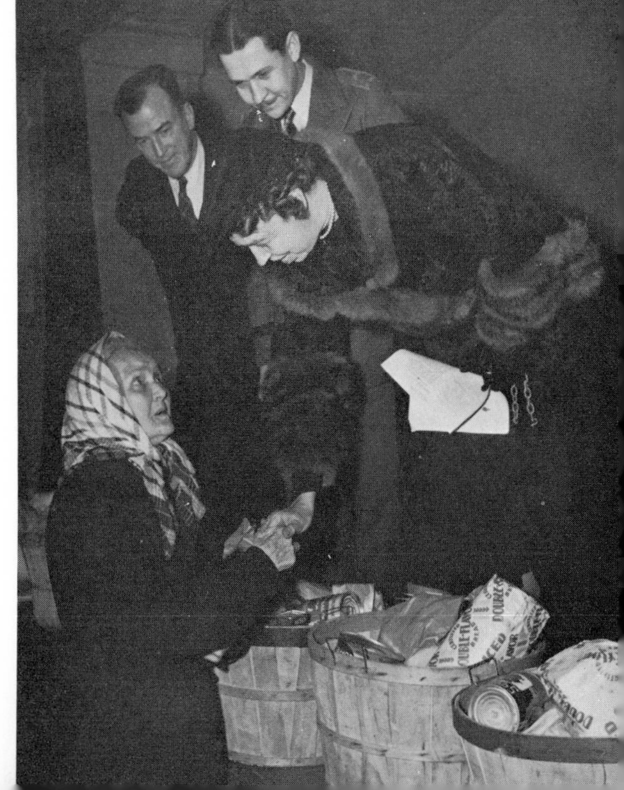

". . . ill nourished. . . ."

As long as she lived, Malvina ("Tommy") Thompson was one of the few who could tell Eleanor Roosevelt, "You didn't put your best efforts into that one." Edith Helm (standing) was the social secretary, but Tommy was the companion, alter ego, screen, and antenna for her friend. "Not only did she always scold me if she felt I did a poor job or spent too little time on something, but she always analyzed people more quickly than I did. Tommy taught me a great deal."

VAL-KILL COTTAGES
HYDE PARK, DUTCHESS COUNTY
NEW YORK

P.P.F 2

For the President:

These two memos were given ~~me by~~ Morris Ernst. Both are excellent. Could you not have them to some one with a little push?

x PPF 2841 x 41-a

Justice Frankfurter might be the one to push the immigration thing, and Mr. Stimson and Mr. Knox might be the ones to decide about the other.

E.R.

x 2 x 18

Rec'd 10/11/40

X

THE WHITE HOUSE
WASHINGTON

February 24, 1941

Dear Harry:

Dr. Henry Pratt Fairchild and Mr. Morris Ernst and a small group had a discussion with me about the importance of having a thorough study of the population situation in the United States, with a view to the formulation of a national policy which would combine the general interests of social welfare with the immediate problem of national welfare.

I suggested a meeting of people who might be interested and your name was among those suggested.

I am having a small, informal dinner here in the White House on March 4 at 7:30 o'clock and hope very much that you will be interested and able to be with us.

Affectionately,

E.R.

After they returned from a trip, any trip, Eleanor dictated and Tommy typed the memos and reports that went to government department heads all over Washington. And if the action didn't come quickly enough on matters she felt vital, she went directly to those who could and would act. The lower letter went to Harry Hopkins, the administrative right hand of the President.

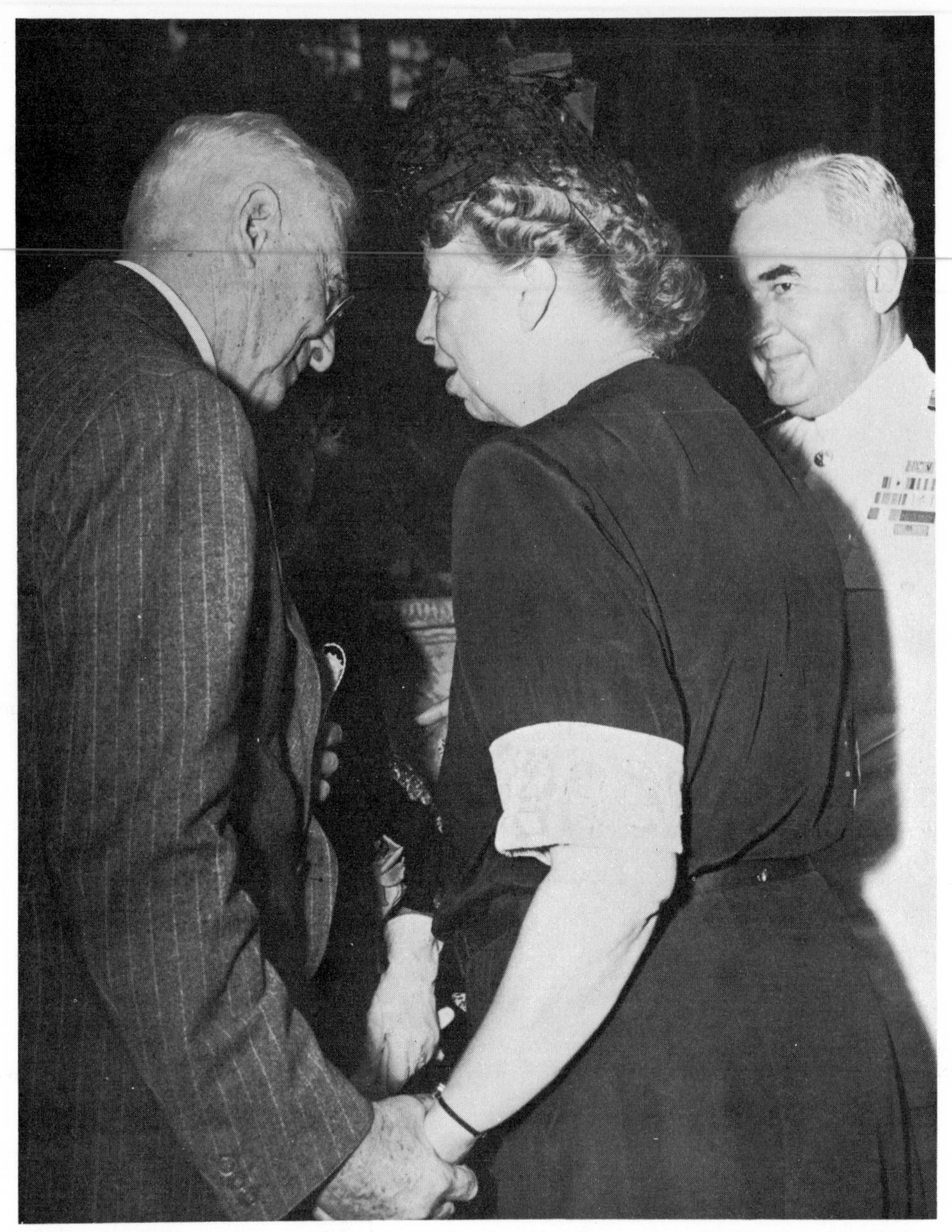

When she believed in something strongly enough, she even pulled in her friends for help. She brought Bernard Baruch to tour the Tygart Valley Housing project in West Virginia to get his advice on proper financing that would tear down tarpaper shacks and put up neat new little homes. Baruch asked about the land cost, and the project people told him: $60 to $100 an acre. Then he wanted to know the house cost: $2,600. And finally he said, "I'd like to see these figures broken down to see if it's possible," and Eleanor Roosevelt answered quickly, "I can give them to you. . . ."

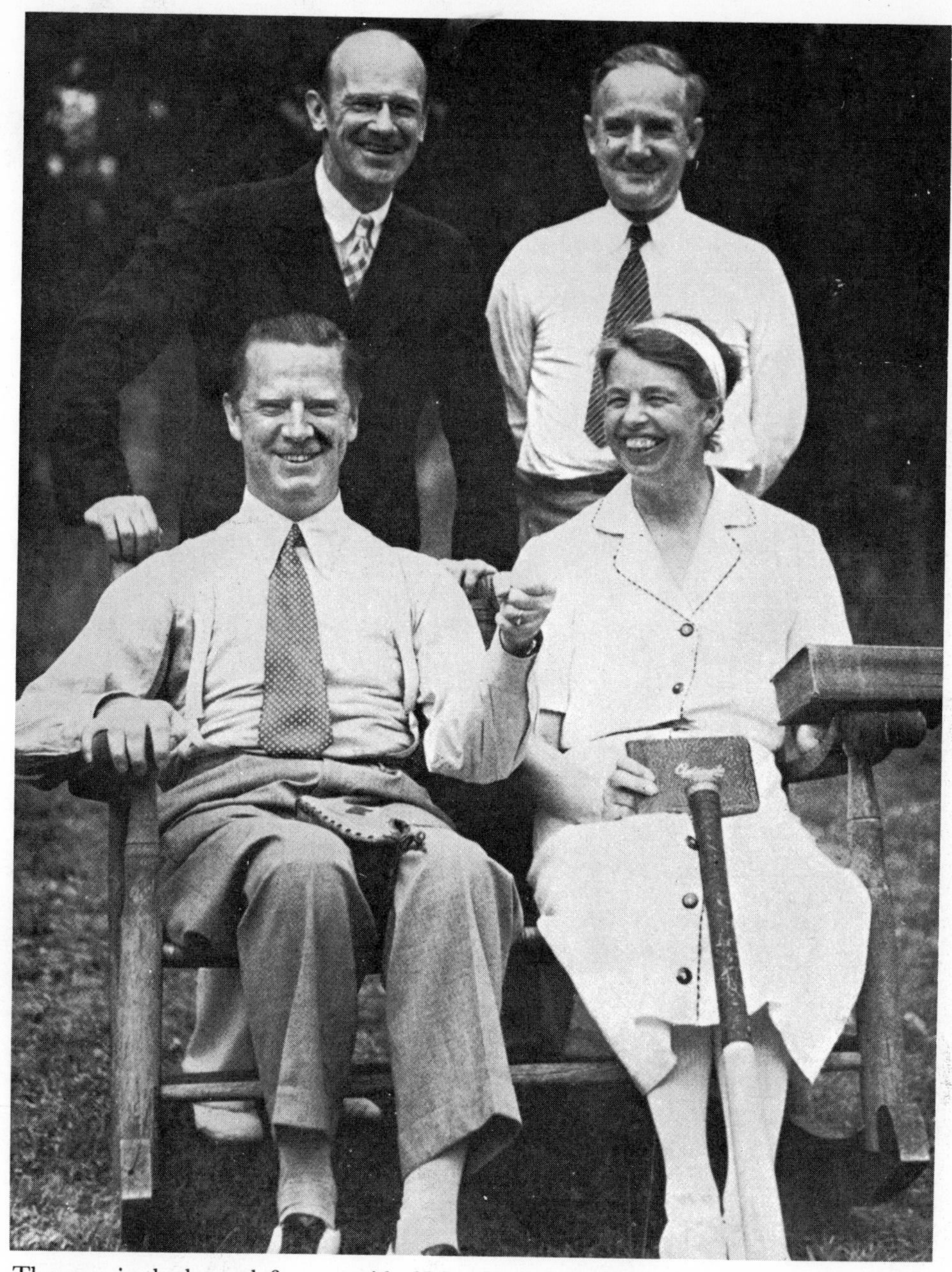

The man in the lower left once said of Mrs. Roosevelt, "I think we can take the wraps off and call her the greatest American woman because there is no other who works as hard or knows the low-down truth about the people and the troubles in their hearts as well as she does. And for what reason? Mrs. Roosevelt doesn't give a damn about politics in the partisan sense." Westbrook Pegler then changed his mind, and wrote, "If we recognize Mrs. Roosevelt as a cunning and persistent politician then we can better understand her moves and protect ourselves against the deception which operates in the guise of a gracious lady of privileged position." Standing (left) Deems Taylor and George Bye, her literary agent.

It was a June day in 1939 and Dr. Will Alexander, director of the Farm Security Administration, arrived at the White House promptly at 9:30 in the morning for his scheduled appointment with Mrs. Roosevelt, whom some FSA officials jokingly called "Migrant Number One." After a forty-minute discussion on sharecropper problems, Mrs. Roosevelt glanced at her watch and excused herself. Twenty minutes later she and the President left the White House to meet the King and Queen of England.

The Queen sat on a car cushion that had springs in it to make it easier for her to keep up with the continual bowing. She so much admired the Queen, who never seemed to have a crease in her dress or a hair out of place. The admiration was mutual. The Queen told her: "I saw in the paper that you were being attacked for having gone to a meeting of the WPA workers. It surprises me that there should be any criticism, for it is so much better to allow people with grievances to air them . . . to someone in whom they feel a sense of sympathy and who may be able to reach the head of government with their grievances."

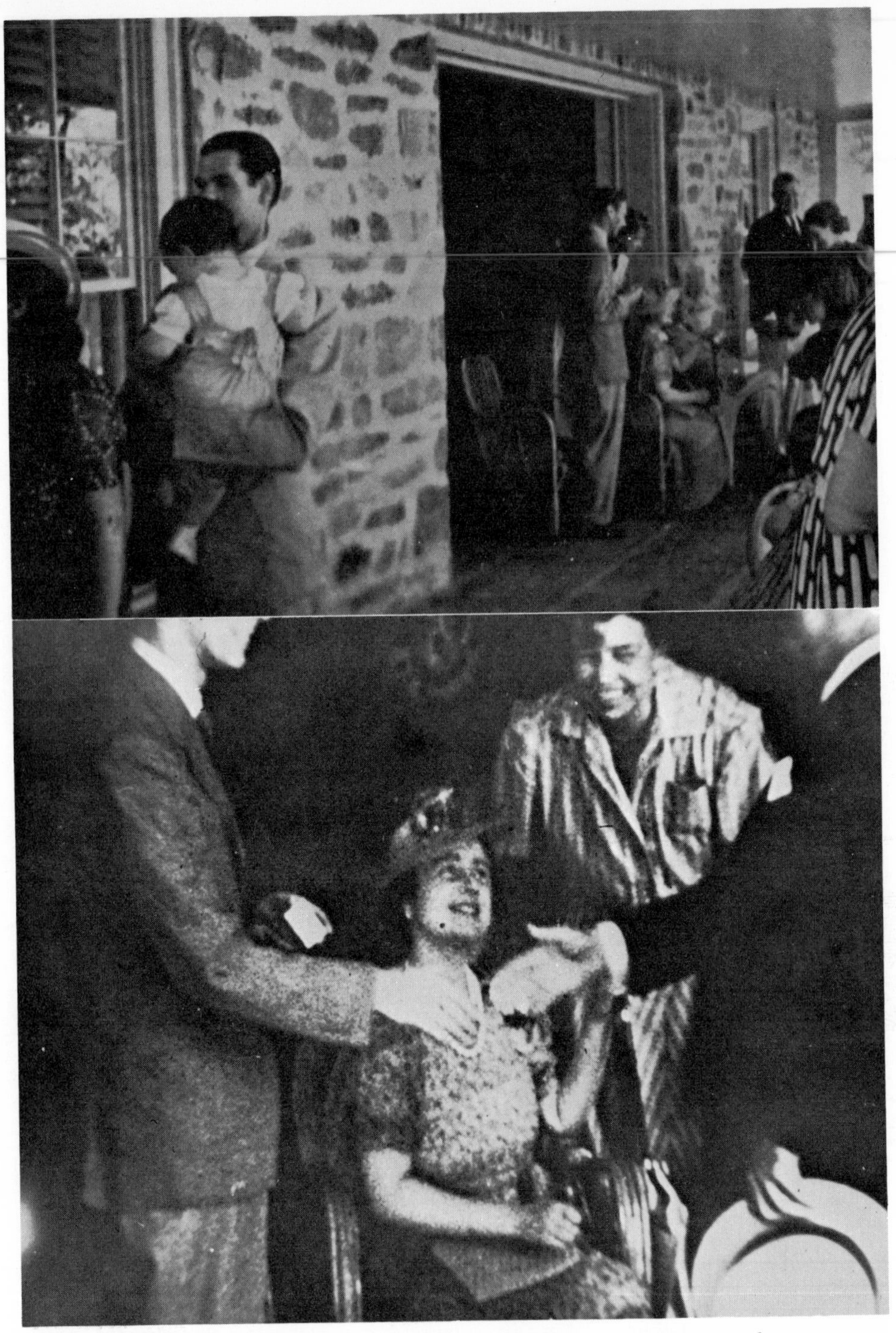

State Department protocol people presented detailed instructions on how to treat royalty—even down to the kind of bathroom supplies. But she had her own ideas that included an informal picnic at Hyde Park featuring American foods—everything from cornpone to hot dogs.

"Things come in threes," said the President, laughing as two waiters crashed down with dishes in front of the royalty. And, sure enough, a third waiter slipped with dishes. Discussing rules for a hostess, she had once written, "Ease is the essential. If accidents occur she is not upset, for she knows that similar things happen in everybody's house." Other entertainment for royalty included the Coon Creek girls of Pinchem-Tight Hollow and some American Indians.

'BUT IT WOULD MAKE SUCH A NICE SCOOP IF YOU'D ONLY TELL ME, FRANKLIN.'
MY DAY
-by-
Eleanor Roosevelt
BURCK
This is the cartoon which so amused Mrs. Franklin D. Roosevelt that she had her secretary write to The Chronicle requesting the original drawing by Burck. It originally appeared in this newspaper April 28 and is being reprinted for the benefit of those who may have missed it two weeks ago.

Prompting this cartoon was the big IF of the Third Term. On other subjects, FDR's secretary Grace Tully reported hearing her boss tell his wife, "Darling, you can't use this in your column—it's off the record." Things her 11,000,000 readers read first in her column, long before the President came out for them publicly, included: proposal for Selective Service; controls of wages as well as prices to combat inflation; over-all manpower controls and limitations of individual income.

She herself didn't want him to run for a third term, kept urging him to prepare a successor, even rented a large apartment for the two of them in New York City. But when he made his decision and asked her to fly to the National Convention in Chicago to smooth political tensions, she went. And she did her job well. But the thing that thrilled her most, and she called it to her friend Lorena Hickok, was, "Hick, they let me fly the plane!"

". . . AND WE DON'T WANT ELEANOR EITHER. . . ." read one of the signs near the White House. But she still worked closely and quietly with Democratic National Chairman Ed Flynn, detailed the plan she had helped originate of a nation-wide web of active units of Democratic women workers. She still made no campaign speeches, in fact, never made any speeches at all when her husband was present. When she was introduced at a Hyde Park festival and they asked for a speech, she answered, "I never make any," and her husband joined in the laughter, and said, "I have just heard my wife say she never makes speeches. Well, live and learn. . . ."

"To make a house a home is still the greatest gift a woman has to give," she once said, "and to make a home under any and all conditions, with whatever is at hand, is genius." It took special genius to make a home out of the White House—where one guard even refused admittance to her son because he drove up in a jalopy and had no proper identification; where a husband cut the budget and then complained about the sameness of food; where curtains, rugs, and furniture were falling apart with no money for replacement; and where the phone might ring with FDR asking her to please get rid of a few guests because "I think we may soon have a few prime ministers."

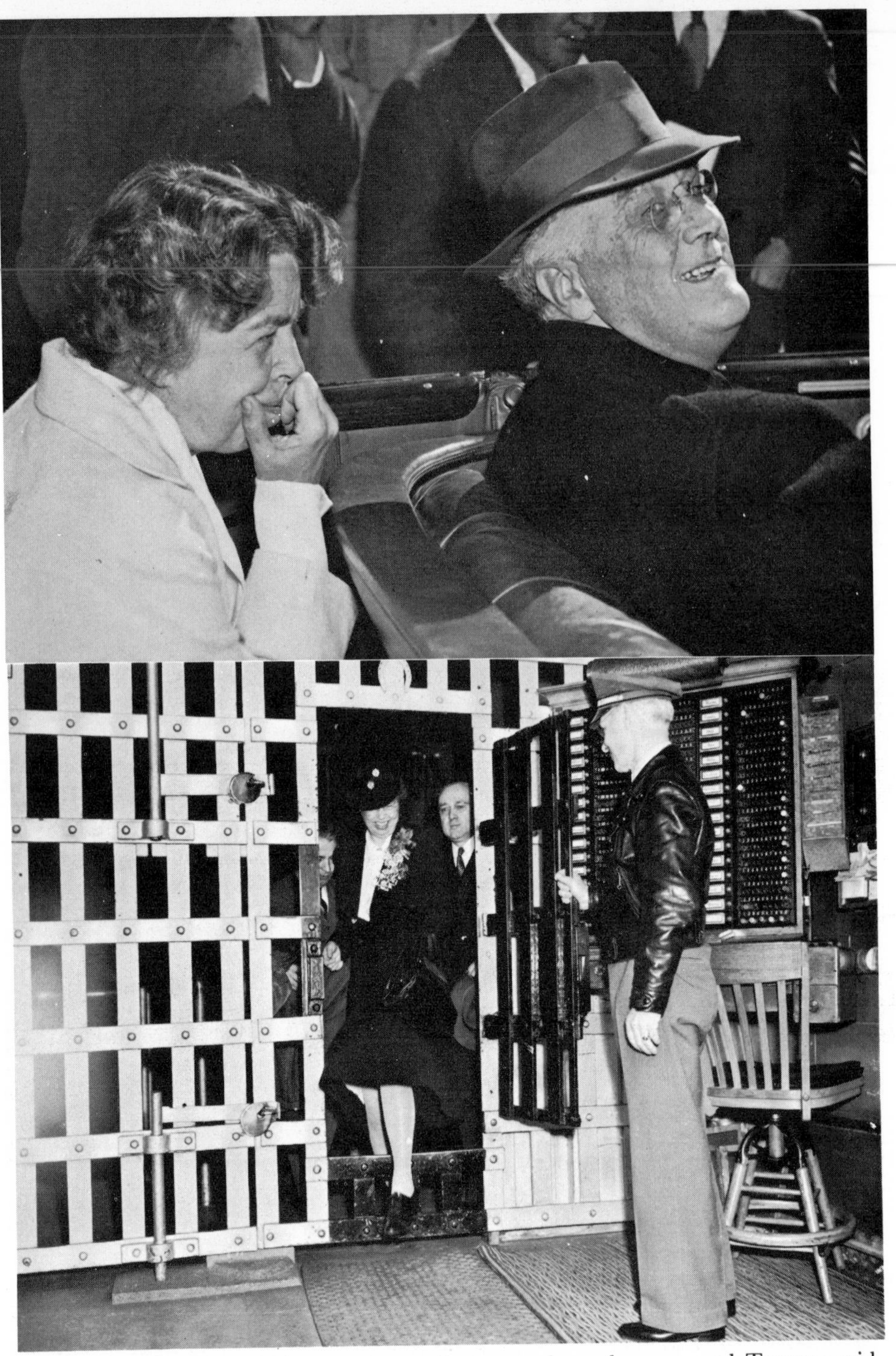

FDR once called his wife's secretary to find out where she was, and Tommy said, "She's in prison, Mr. President." FDR had a quick comeback, "I'm not surprised," he said, "but what for?"

They named a color after her, Eleanor Blue (her favorite), and they also named in her honor, dolls, housing projects, roses, and even a dance. The dance was the "Eleanor Glide," created and danced by her protégée Mayris Chaney. The press pounced on Miss Chaney. Years later, they pounced again when Mrs. Roosevelt appointed her to the job of Director of Physical Fitness in the Office of Civilian Defense. Both she and Mrs. Roosevelt resigned from the OCD.

THE WHITE HOUSE
WASHINGTON

January 16, 1941

MEMORANDUM FOR

HON. ROBERT PATTERSON

What shall I tell Mrs.

Roosevelt about this?

xPP72

F. D. R./tab

Enclosure

Memorandum for the President from Mrs. Roosevelt in re appt. of women to Army Committee on Community Service for the Army camps.

THE WHITE HOUSE

WASHINGTON

MEMO FOR THE PRESIDENT

It has been called to my attention that the Army has appointed a committee on Community Service for the Army camps.

This is a committee of 7, and 5 members are civilian men, and 2 are Army officers.

The feeling is that this is a committee on which a woman or women could well have been appointed.

When some one in the War Department was asked about it - he replied that "it had never occured to him!

E.R.

When somebody asked her, "What have women done with the vote?" she had a ready answer: "I often wonder why men are not asked the same question." Still, she felt strongly that women had not fulfilled their political potential, that sex was still a basis of judgment in giving government jobs, and she fought it hard wherever she could.

War came with Pearl Harbor, and hate against anything Japanese mounted to hysteria. Yet the day after Pearl Harbor, she flew to Seattle, posed with four Nisei, pleading in the press that these loyal American citizens of Japanese descent be treated with neighborliness and the American sense of fair play. But they weren't. And when these American citizens—who later proved their loyalty as soldiers in combat—were herded into camps, she was the first to visit them and voice her sense of national shame.

Like other mothers, she watched her sons go to war: John and Franklin, Jr., to the Navy, James to the Marines, Elliott to the Air Force—all of them in combat. And, still, there were all kinds of cranks who wrote her: "I hope all your sons get killed."

She added a new family of three foster children: four-year-old Tommy, son of a coal stoker in London; fourteen-year-old Spanish Kerman Garale; and seventeen-year-old Polish Janina Dybowska. For all war orphan refugee children, she pleaded with Congress to let them into this country. One Congressman said he wasn't going to let the President tell him what to do, and certainly not his wife. The bill didn't pass.

The invasion of North Africa was soon scheduled, and her husband wanted her to go to England and see the troops. She packed one evening dress, two day dresses, one suit, a few blouses, one pair of day shoes, and one pair of evening shoes—all of which looked skimpy in the huge Buckingham Palace closet. Her code name was apt—"Rover." Among those meeting her at the train were the King and Queen, the American Ambassador, and a general named Dwight D. Eisenhower.

She saw what war was, sampled the blackout, witnessed the bomb damage, traveled in open trucks, wore out trailing reporters, visited all the hospitals, sang with the soldiers, talked to people living in air-raid shelters and subways, and even managed a short reunion with her old classmates of Allenswood School in Surrey. There was a quibble on return transportation, and her husband cabled, "I don't care how you send her, just send her."

Reaction to her British trip was good enough—especially among soldiers themselves—so that FDR asked her to tour the Caribbean and then the Pacific and "see as many of the men as you can and see how things are going with them." Just as in England, she concentrated on the miles and miles of hospital wards. One fat colonel, puffing to keep up with her, interrupted to say that they were already late for a lunch with some Very Important People. She simply smiled and said, "Just one more ward, colonel. . . ."

She traveled 25,000 miles, stopped at seventeen islands including Australia and New Zealand, lost twenty-five pounds, averaged five hours' sleep, and filled fat notebooks with names and addresses of mothers, wives, sweethearts of soldiers whom she later wrote to or called. One thing she was grateful for: she had traveled so much in the United States that she could talk knowingly to so many soldiers about their home towns and watch their faces light up.

Drawn in 1942 by Herblock at the time of the British commando raid on Dieppe, for NEA Service.

She made friends everywhere she went.

Back home the Penobscot Indians of Maine pinpointed her with the title of "Ow-du-sees-ul," which translated as "Princess of Many Trails." An Indian princess placed the wampum around her head and said, "My song is for your protection on your many trails."

". . . The Republican leaders have not been content with attacks on me, or my wife, or on my sons . . . they now include my little dog Fala. . . ." Queen Juliana of the Netherlands is seated next to Mrs. Roosevelt.

To prove his physical fitness for the fourth term, FDR drove the fifty miles through New York City in the driving rain in an open car, drenching both him and his wife. The trip did give him a chance to see, for the first time, the apartment his wife had rented and furnished for the two of them, an apartment they would never use together.

FDR was his ebullient self at the traditional Hyde Park torchlight parade of victory. But his wife knew his tiredness, worried about him. She had wanted to go with him to Yalta, but he wouldn't take her because he said none of the other wives would be there. But he did take his daughter Anna, standing here behind him.

Thirteen grandchildren, all in one room—their last family picture together.

It was at a meeting of the Red Cross Hospital Entertainment Committee at the Sulgrave Hotel when Mary Howard greeted her, the last time she was photographed before the call came from White House Press Secretary Steve Early. He simply told her to hurry home, not telling her why, but she felt it, she knew. Still, she said good-by to her hostess and sat in the car with clenched hands all the way to the White House.

She followed her husband into the White House for the last time. "Somehow, one moves automatically," she said afterward. She looked around the East Room and remembered, "It seemed as if everybody in the world was there except three of my own sons." They were still in combat. At the funeral service, she asked the bishop to repeat the phrase from her husband's 1933 inaugural message, "The only thing we have to fear is fear itself." She was then on her own.

P.P.7. 7

THE WHITE HOUSE
WASHINGTON

April 16, 1945

file

My dear Mr. President:

There have been many thousands of letters, telegrams and cards sent to me and my children which have brought great comfort and consolation to all of us. This outpouring of affectionate thought has touched us all deeply and we wish it were possible to thank each and everyone individually.

My children and I feel in view of the fact that we are faced with a paper shortage and are asked not to use paper when it can be avoided, that all we can do is to express our appreciation collectively. We would therefore consider it a great favor if you would be kind enough to express our gratitude for us.

Sincerely yours,

Eleanor Roosevelt

6. The World Citizen

The first memorial service for FDR was held in the rose garden of his Hyde Park home near the simple stone monument that marks his grave. It was a quiet ceremony with few speeches and much feeling, and Eleanor Roosevelt told the people how much Hyde Park meant to her husband and to her. When it was over most people scattered, but many kept crowding into the house, now a national museum, filtering into the various rooms, standing quietly behind wooden rails, staring at the things which used to be his: the shelves of books, the long desk, the pictures of old sailing ships, the boyhood collection of birds, the bed in which he was born, the small-looking wheel chair in a corner.

A mother and her small son came in and the mother was explaining that this was the library of President Roosevelt, who had died the year before. The little boy looked quickly around the room, his eyes lighting on the five small framed pictures of Fala.

"Is that his dog, Mama?"

His mother nodded.

"Did his dog die, too?"

Fala was always waiting for his master to come back, but Eleanor Roosevelt, alone now, knew she must look forward. It had been a year of adjustment, work, decisions, and loneliness. She had made her plans. There would be no more living in the big Hyde Park house with a staff of servants. She was now residing in a cottage renovated from her furniture factory on a wooded parcel of land beside the Val Kill Creek deeded to her by her husband years before. There in a house she had planned herself, furnished with the simplest possessions and family heirlooms, surrounded by pictures and mementos of those she loved, she prepared to live a quiet life and one of service.

Service is the key to her core. She herself told a friend, "Think of it! I am over sixty, which means I only have fifteen years left of useful public service."

The chance for this came quickly.

"I was with her when the phone rang," said her son Franklin, Jr. "It was President Truman and he was asking her to be the United States representative to the United Nations, and she automatically answered, 'But I don't know anything about parliamentary procedure. . . .'

"President Truman asked her to think about it and let him know, and when she hung up, we discussed it. What she said was that, after all, even though she had acted as the eyes and ears for Father and had brought her information back to him, the final decision was always his. She could and would discuss it with him, even argue with him, but it was his decision, and, once made, she would rely and depend on it. Now, with Father gone, if she accepted this position, she would have to make her own decisions, and many of them would be important ones."

Franklin urged her to do it. So did everybody else.

"And so when Mother took that job," said Franklin, "I felt that it was a real kind of turning point in her life. She was now on her own, I mean really on her own."

Not only did she learn parliamentary procedure, but she learned exactly when to bang a gavel. Representing the United States on the Human Rights Commission meeting in England, she did her utmost to work with the Russians, understand them, get them to compromise on issues. She even invited small groups of them to have tea with her, trying to break through the official pose and find the human beings. But she found their pose too persistent. Again and again at UN meetings she heard the Russians repeat their same points in long-winded speeches that added up to nothing, speeches that were always played for propaganda only. Finally, she decided that she could only fight their ideas, not change them.

Using sharp facts to fight fiction and banging the gavel freely, she shamed many of the Soviet speakers into short speeches, and they found it hard to fight her prestige and her honesty. Even Molotov shied away from debating with her. And her persistence matched theirs—she never missed a single meeting, even though she had a drawn-out, painful case of shingles at one time which would have bedded most people. The final success of the Declaration of Human Rights was her success.

Along with her on that UN delegation were Senator Tom Connally, John Foster Dulles, and Senator Arthur Vandenberg. All of them had been reluctant to serve with her, particularly Vandenberg, who had complained loudly about it to congressional Republican friends. Columnist Doris Fleeson tells the story of Vandenberg's return to Washington and somebody saying, "How did you get along with Eleanor?" Vandenberg snapped back, "I've said a lot of mean things about Mrs. Roosevelt, but I want to tell you now that I take them all back. She's a grand person and a great American citizen."

And the Dowager Marchioness of Reading, head of the Women's Voluntary Service in London, said: "Eleanor Roosevelt cares first and always for people . . . her interest is human beings, her hobby is human beings, her preoccupation is human beings, and her every thought is for human beings. As every single thing she devotes herself to has to do with human beings of one sort or another, I believe that the basis of all her strength is in her profound interest in them and her readiness to share with them the agony of experience, and the fulfillment of destiny."

Her value was not fully appreciated, however, by the incoming Republican administration, which promptly retired her from the UN, but only as a delegate. As a citizen she kept her UN interest as a purposeful part of her life, joining the American Association for the UN, speaking everywhere to promote it, educate citizens about it, and get increased support for it.

"What I can't understand," she said, "is why so much of the press and the public have been attacking the United Nations instead of supporting it. Doesn't everybody know by now that the United Nations is our last big hope for peace in the world?"

In accepting a position with the UN she had decided against taking an active part in politics. In 1948 President Truman publicly stated that he would be very glad to have Mrs. Roosevelt run as vice-president with him, and in 1946 Democratic boss Ed Flynn made her a straight offer: Democratic nomination for the United States Senate.

This gave her a chance to be a part of the national planning, a chance to become a political showcase for the women of the world, a chance to serve her political party and her government in the fullest sense.

She refused. She felt her duty was with the United Nations. She also felt she could serve her party more strongly from the side lines. And there is no question about her strength.

Her support for Adlai Stevenson in 1952 pulled many people to his side when he was still unknown, and she probably convinced Truman. And when Truman changed his mind in 1956 and switched to Harriman at the convention, Eleanor Roosevelt unquestionably helped turned the tide in Stevenson's favor when she postponed a trip to Europe with her grandsons so that she could add her weight to the political pressure to get him nominated.

On returning from abroad, she followed a strenuous campaign schedule of speeches and appearances in support of Stevenson, touring in an open car in all kinds of weather, catching midnight trains, and flying from one end of the country to the other—and she was then past the age of seventy.

And even now she still keeps two full-time secretaries busy, replying to fifty invitations a day to speak somewhere, and answering a hundred letters a day from people pleading causes, asking favors, and seeking her advice. She also continues to write her daily column, makes scores of radio and TV appearances, fulfills book contracts, prepares magazine articles, gives lectures, addresses groups all over the country, and entertains her family and friends.

She travels everywhere. If the big Hyde Park house is too large for her to live in, the world is now her house: England, to see her husband's memorial statue unveiled, this one standing straight and strong as a young wife once remembered him; the Middle East, where she refused the offer of an Arab sheik, who wanted her to join his harem; India, where she saw pitiful poverty and great hopes; Japan, where the women personified her as feminine freedom and carefully asked her views on everything from mothers-in-law to Hiroshima; Hong Kong, where she discovered that her uncle really did cargo some opium (as did nearly everyone else) in the China trade; Yugoslavia, where she differed with Marshal Tito and told him frankly, "I am not sure that this proves that the Yugoslav Government will not return to closer ties with Moscow when you are stronger and no longer need our help"; and Russia, where she found a country of frightening discipline, a people without laughter. After she had talked forthrightly with Khrushchev at Yalta, he asked if he could tell the press that they had had a friendly conversation. "Yes," she replied, "if you will add that we differed on many things."

Wherever she goes she buys presents to be brought back to her home in Hyde Park, ticketed, docketed, and tucked away in a spacious cupboard reserved for the purpose till Christmas when all possible members of the family, young and old, gather from far and wide, to celebrate with gifts and feasting. The same tone applies to birthdays, always great occasions in the Roosevelt family. There was a time that the grown-up schedule was so tight and the birthday child had to be taken to town so that the only available hour for the party was at breakfast. And so the child and his friends were all invited for nine in the morning, and after scrambled eggs and fruit juice the birthday cake was brought in appropriately lighted. There were presents for every child and Mrs. Roosevelt had prepared them all, getting up at six o'clock to wrap and mark them herself with favors she had bought at so many places.

Whenever she stops traveling the world, the great and the

humble of the world come to see her. The Churchills, Emperor Haile Selassie, Queen Juliana and Prince Bernhard of the Netherlands, Premier Nehru and Madame Pandit of India, Cardinal Spellman, President Truman, Dowager Queen Mary of England, the King and Queen of Greece, presidents and premiers of many foreign countries, and leaders of American thought have visited her at her cottage in Hyde Park. She has also received international student groups and representatives of American college organizations trying to find their way in a confused political scene, coming to call on her to discuss their problems. In the summer months there are outdoor luncheons beside her swimming pool for visiting dignitaries, and always constant picnics complete with hot dogs for welfare groups, for delegations from foreign countries, for the UN, for underprivileged children, and for her grandchildren and neighbors.

She begins her real "My Day" at seven-thirty in the morning when she is usually awakened by her Scotties clamoring for a walk—before Fala died he used to rub his back against the springs of the bed until he woke her up. After the morning walk, which she takes in sunshine or rain, snow or sleet, there is breakfast at eight-thirty promptly—the beginning of her tight and heavy program for the day which often ends long after midnight.

In the summer months, after she finishes her column in the afternoon and just before tea, there is a daily dive off the springboard into the pool. "It's not that I always enjoy it when the day is chilly," admits Mrs. Roosevelt, "but I think it is good for my character."

After tea she reads fairy tales to her grandchildren and their friends, and then there may be a dozen people for dinner. On weekends there is always a houseful of guests. And on Sundays she attends the eleven-o'clock service at St. James Episcopal church in the village.

When not traveling or staying at Hyde Park she lives in her small apartment in New York City in the East Sixties where she entertains as simply but as generously as she does in the country.

"Mrs. Roosevelt is first and foremost and always a woman," said the Dowager Marchioness of Reading, an old and close friend. "She never transgresses by trying to pretend that she is something quite different to what she is, and never forgets the difficulties she herself has met. That, *to me*, is the test of her greatness.

"I know that when I think of Eleanor Roosevelt I think of someone who gives a very unusual thing by her presence. Having been with her, one leaves her the better ready to undertake one's own life and one's own responsibilities with a determination to have the courage that is hers and to put in operation the strength of purpose that she possesses.

"I believe," her friend concluded, "it could truly be said of this truly great woman that she is not only an example to us all but that in her womanliness she has a heart that never hardens, a touch that never hurts, and a smile that never tires."

"The only limit to our realization of tomorrow will be our doubts of today. Let us move forward with strong and active faith."

These were the last words written by her husband and Eleanor Roosevelt always lived by them.

. . . with the small suitcase ready, the taxi waiting, and the plane warming up to take her forward.

Fala refused to accept the inevitable, and his ears perked up every time some car came up sounding its sirens. But Eleanor Roosevelt spent a quiet summer adjusting herself to a future that seemed quiet.

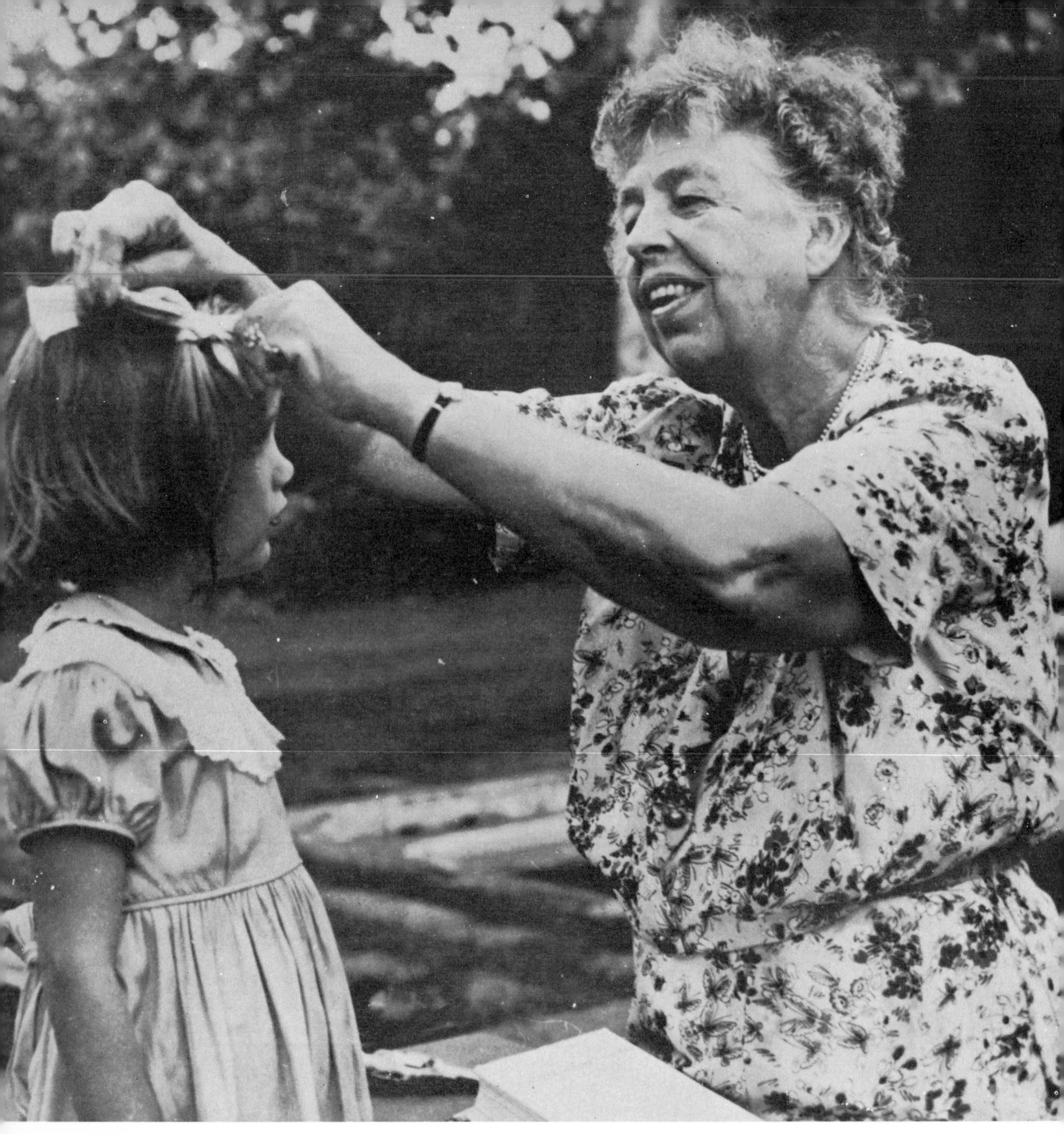

Grandchildren need their bows straightened, their tradition taught. She took a group of them to the deserted house at nearby Tivoli, where she grew up as a girl. And as she led the way through the creaky, empty house, she tried to make it come alive again for them with faces and voices and history. It was almost as if she again could hear her own grandmother tell her, "You are a girl and I expect you to be more sensible than boys."

President Truman telephoned her at home, asking her to become the United States representative to the United Nations and her first answer was, "But I don't know anything about parliamentary procedure. . . ."

A daily column, a hundred letters a day, fifty lectures a year, 50,000 traveling miles—all this and the UN, too, and she never missed a single session, even with a bad case of shingles, which makes it tough even to sit still. Answering a reporter, she said, "I have nothing to do *but* work. I have no family responsibilities, no professional career." Her cousins, the Alsop columnists, had once referred to "that damned Roosevelt extra gland."

They put her on the Human Rights Commission, and she learned how to gavel the Russians into silence. "This is no place for propaganda speeches," she once told them, combining fury with formality, "and I must ask you to draw your remarks to a close."

Passage of the Universal Declaration of Human Rights was almost a personal victory of persistence. The headline on the *New York Times*'s editorial read, "*ELEANOR ROOSEVELT'S VICTORY.*" And it soon became more than mere words: both the new Indian and Indonesian constitutions modeled themselves after the Declaration, and U.S. Federal courts soon referred to it in some of their decisions.

This picture was made during the invocation at a memorial dinner for FDR. Left to right: Supreme Court Justice Hugo L. Black, Mrs. Roosevelt, and Henry Morgenthau, Jr., a long-time family friend and FDR's Secretary of the Treasury. If the phrase "Freedom from Want" expressed an important principle for FDR, it was equally a motivating force for his wife: the fight for this freedom has always been basic to everything she tried to do.

On the go again. Somebody called her "a jet plane with the fringe on top."

Here she is at another FDR memorial service, this one at the American Church of Avenue George V in Paris. Long before, she had written: "Religious training was not just an affair of Sundays—there were family prayers every morning, and you grew up with the feeling that you had a share in some great spiritual existence beyond the everyday round of happenings."

She found her husband almost everywhere. Here a King of England helped her unveil a statue in Grosvenor Square before the hush of a huge crowd.

Setting the pace again, this time accompanied by one of her dearest friends, the Dowager Marchioness of Reading (extreme left), head of the Women's Land Army in Britain.

Sir Winston Churchill had a question to ask her in England: "You don't really approve of me, do you, Mrs. Roosevelt?" And she didn't. During his wartime trips to Washington, he had kept her husband up almost to the dawning hours, then slept late while FDR had to get up early for his full day.

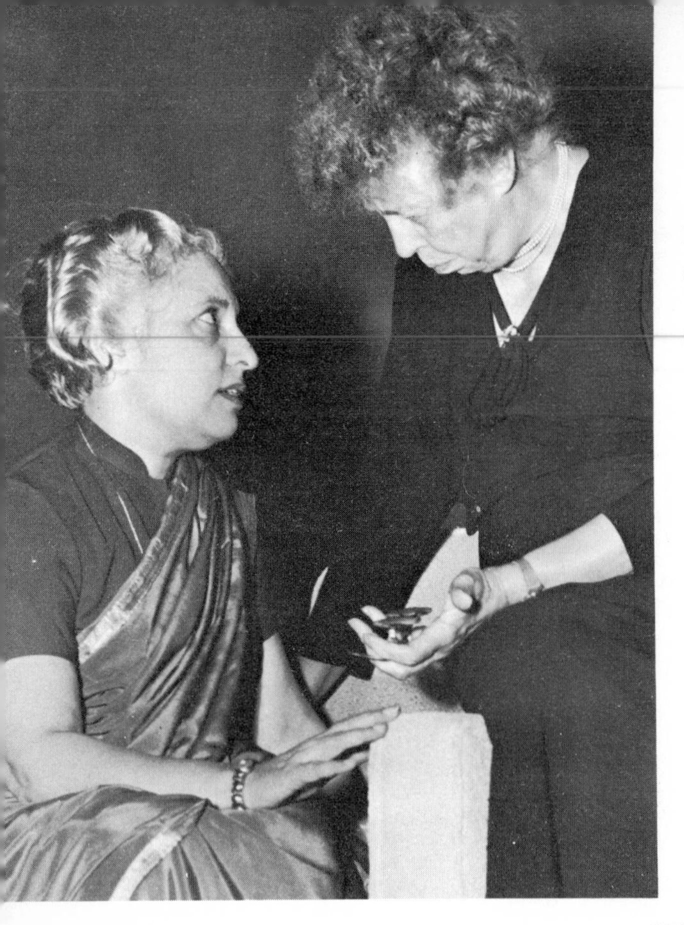

Mme. Vijaya Lakshmi Pandit, once Indian Ambassador to the United States and former chairman of the UN General Assembly, listens intently to a double image: the woman best known and the American most respected in Asia and Africa because of her strong stand on Civil Rights.

After sight-seeing the tiny Dutch island of Tholen, where the founder of the American Roosevelt family once lived, she then visited the Netherlands' Queen Juliana, who stayed with her often at Hyde Park. FDR was godfather of Juliana's third child.

This Arab Sheikh Suleiman Ali es Sayid was seventy years old and had thirty-nine wives in his harem, but he liked Eleanor Roosevelt just fine and gave her the present of a silver dagger, which was his way of proposing that she join his harem as wife number forty. But she didn't realize that until later.

She spirited Queen Frederika of Greece away from the State Department long enough to show her things she really wanted to see: rehabilitation hospitals and the way firemen slide down the pole in a firehouse.

FDR in Oslo looked out at Norwegian fjords, a granite statue with the scroll of the Atlantic Charter in his hand. "My husband loved the sea," she told the people, "and he loved sailboats just like the people of Norway."

She had her two grandsons with her in Denmark, where she unveiled still another sculptured tribute to her husband, this one also paid for by the public. Many years before, she had taken two of her sons on a similar European trip and vowed never to do it again. But nobody feels more deeply the value of travel for children, "because there is fearfully lacking in them a sense of dignity of other people in other countries."

These are Jewish children from Morocco, soon to be Israeli citizens. Being with these Old Testament children may have recalled her favorite section of the New Testament, I Corinthians 13: "Though I speak with the tongues of men and angels, and have not charity, I am become as sounding brass, or a tinkling cymbal."

These Swedish children can recognize somebody's grandmother when they see one.

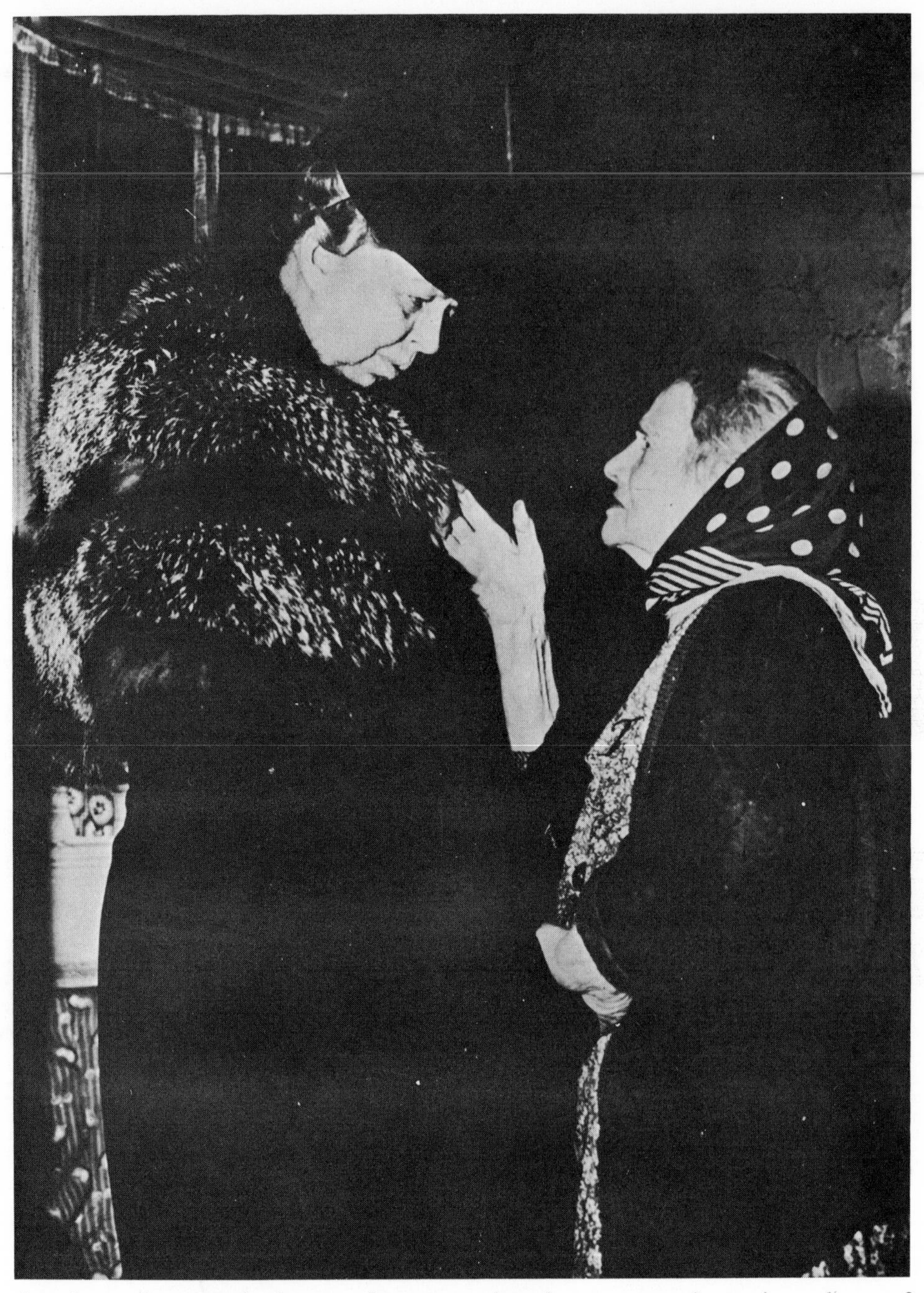

Age demands sympathetic ears of age even though one woman's age is made up of time and the other has young years made of spirit and speed.

It didn't matter how you went, as long as you got there.

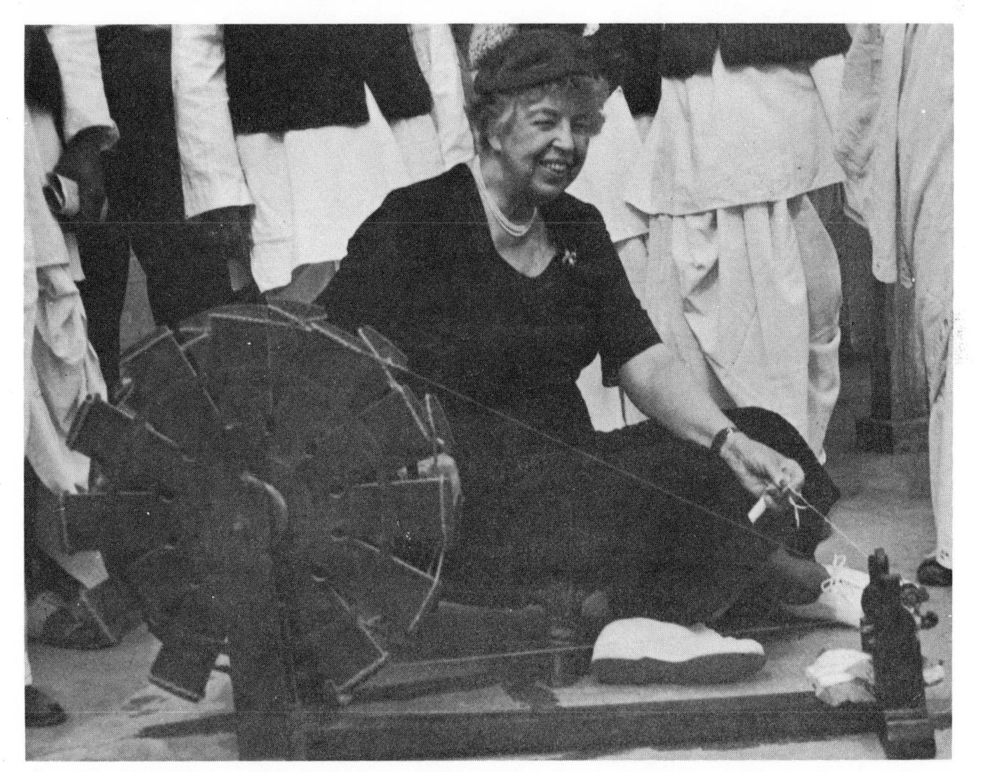

One is never too old to learn—even though she never did go to college except to take a cooking course at Columbia University.

Some tourists only see the Taj Mahal in moonlight and think they see India. How many see the child labor in the hosiery section of the Faridabad Colony?

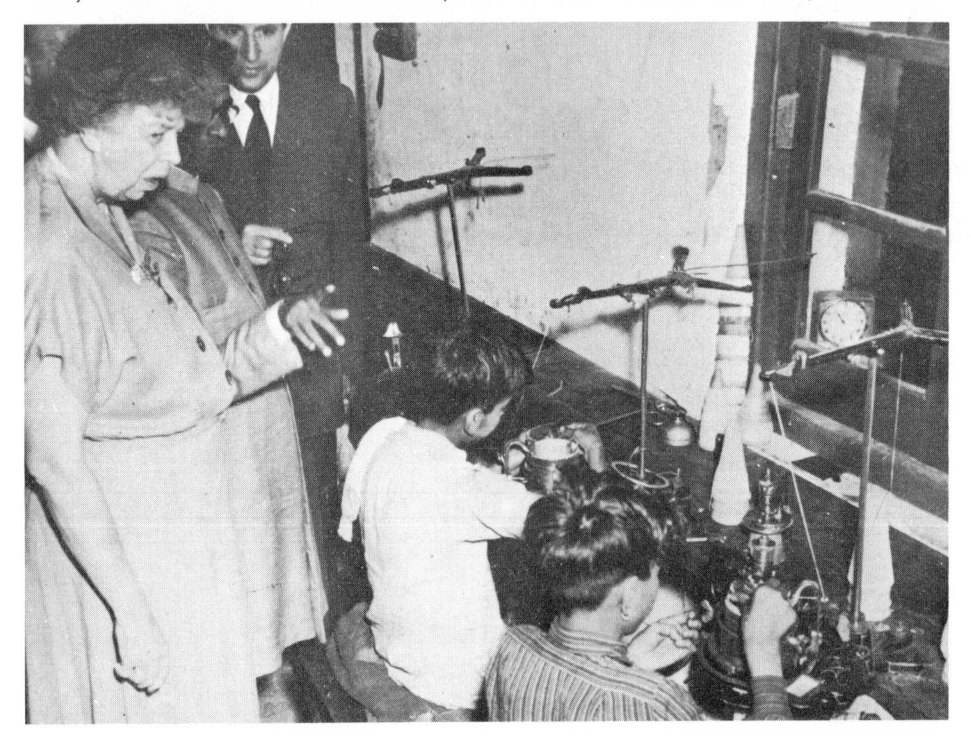

Travel brings understanding, and here she brings an active understanding of western folk dancing to the people of Pakistan. An Office of War Information profile some time ago claimed she was also an expert in the rumba.

More west to east is her narration of *Peter and the Wolf*, which she did once before with the Boston Symphony Orchestra, and here with a Japanese symphony orchestra in Tokyo.

File

Tentative Schedule for Mrs. Roosevelt

(Subject to change)
May 22 - May 31, 1953

May 22, Friday	
12:30 p.m.	Arrive at Haneda, PAA, No. 5
Hotel in Tokyo:	Imperial Hotel Press interview at the Imperial Hotel lobby (2 hours after the arrival: for 30 minutes) Miss Matsuoka, interpreter
Contact Person:	Miss Kiyoko Takeda, Mrs. Roosevelt Program Committee, Room 206, Imperial Hotel Kokusai Bunka Kaikan (international House of Japan), Togin Bldg., Marunouchi, Tel: 23-6128, 6129
afternoon	Free
evening	Free
May 23, Saturday	
morning	Free
12:00a.m.	Leave Hotel for Korin-Kaku
12:15a.m.	Welcome Lunchion by the Committee for Intellectual Interchange and International House of Japan at Korin-Kaku
2;15p.m.	Leave Korin-Kaku for Imperial Hotel
2;45p.m.	Leave Imperial Hotel for Sengoku Villa (Mr. & Mrs. Griffith)
5;15p.m.	Arrive Sengoku Villa
evening	Dinner and round table discussion (No.1) on "Patterns of Japanese Life and Culture"
May 24, Sunday	
morning	
3;00p.m.	Leave Sengoku Villa for Kugenuma
4;15p.m.	Arrive at Villa of Princess Chichibu at Kugenuma
5;35p.m.	Leave " " " for Tokyo
7;00p.m.	Arrive at Imperial Hotel
May 25, Monday	
10;20a.m.	Leave for Tokyo Army Hospital (Col. Kirkpatrick will call at the Hotel at 10;15a.m.)
10;30-11;30a.m.	Visit to Tokyo Army Hospital
11;45a.m.	Return to the Hotel
12;00a.m.	Leave the Hotel for Kyosai-Kaikan
12;10-2;45p.m.	Round table discussion (NO.2) on "Status of Women in Japan" sponsored by Women's and Minor's Bureau, Ministry of Labour (Miss Taki(Miss Taki Fujita, Chidf of Women's and Minors' bureau, in chair): lunch
2;45p.m.	Leave for Tokyo-Kaikan
3;00-4;30p.m.	Address to members of Tokyo Women's Club, followed by reception at Tokyo Kaikan (Mrs. Cooper Blythe, President of the Club)
4;30p.m.	Leave Tokyo Kaikan for Hotel
4;45-7;00p.m.	Rest
7;00-9;30p.m.	Supper and round table discussion (NO.3) on "Patterns of Japanese Life and Culture"

"I have never been bored. . . ."

"I have always been curious. . . ."

No matter what the country, crippled children have a common language. It is a language she understood a long time ago. She learned it first from her father, later from her husband.

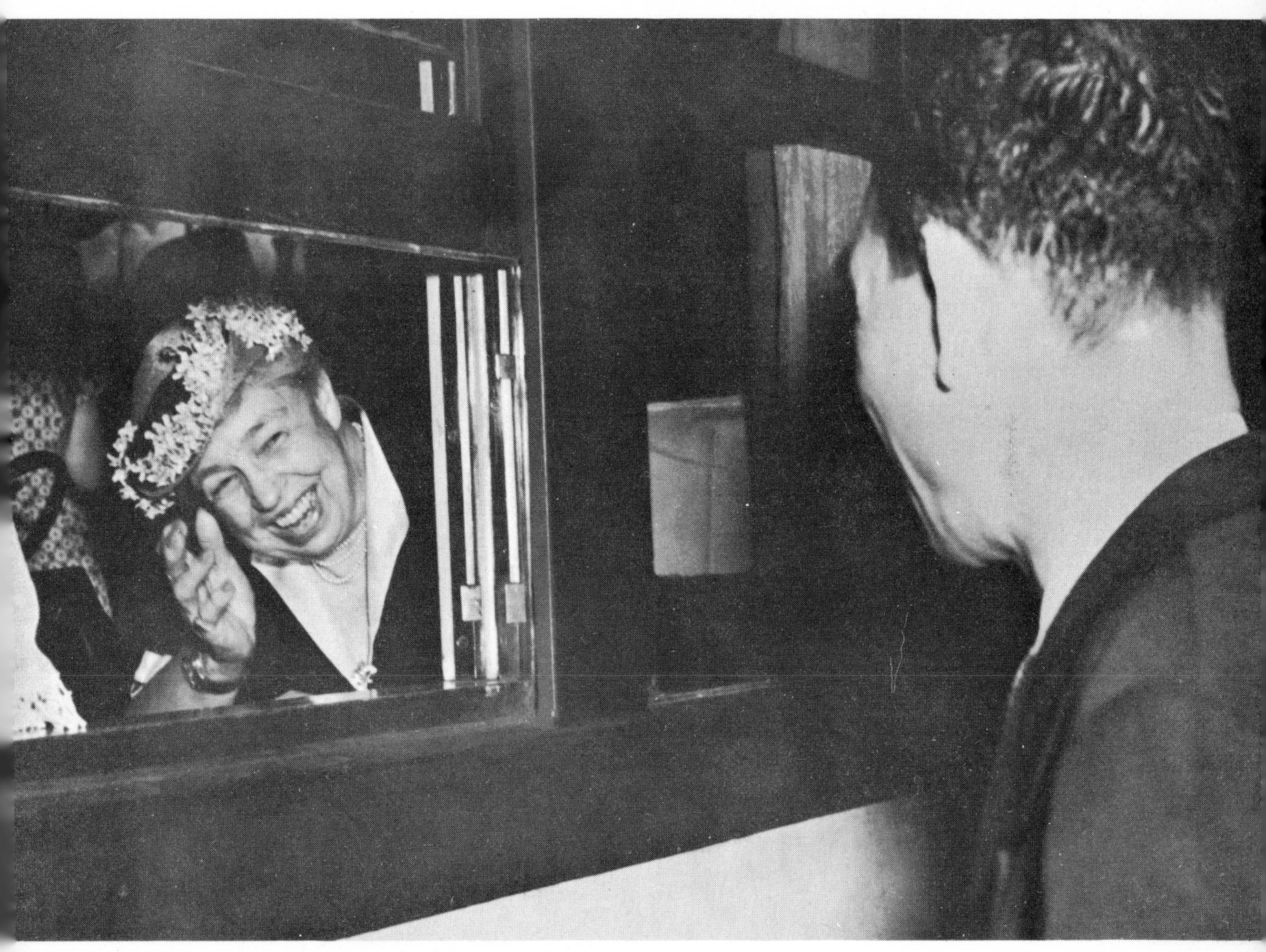

Sayonara to Japan and hello, Hyde Park.

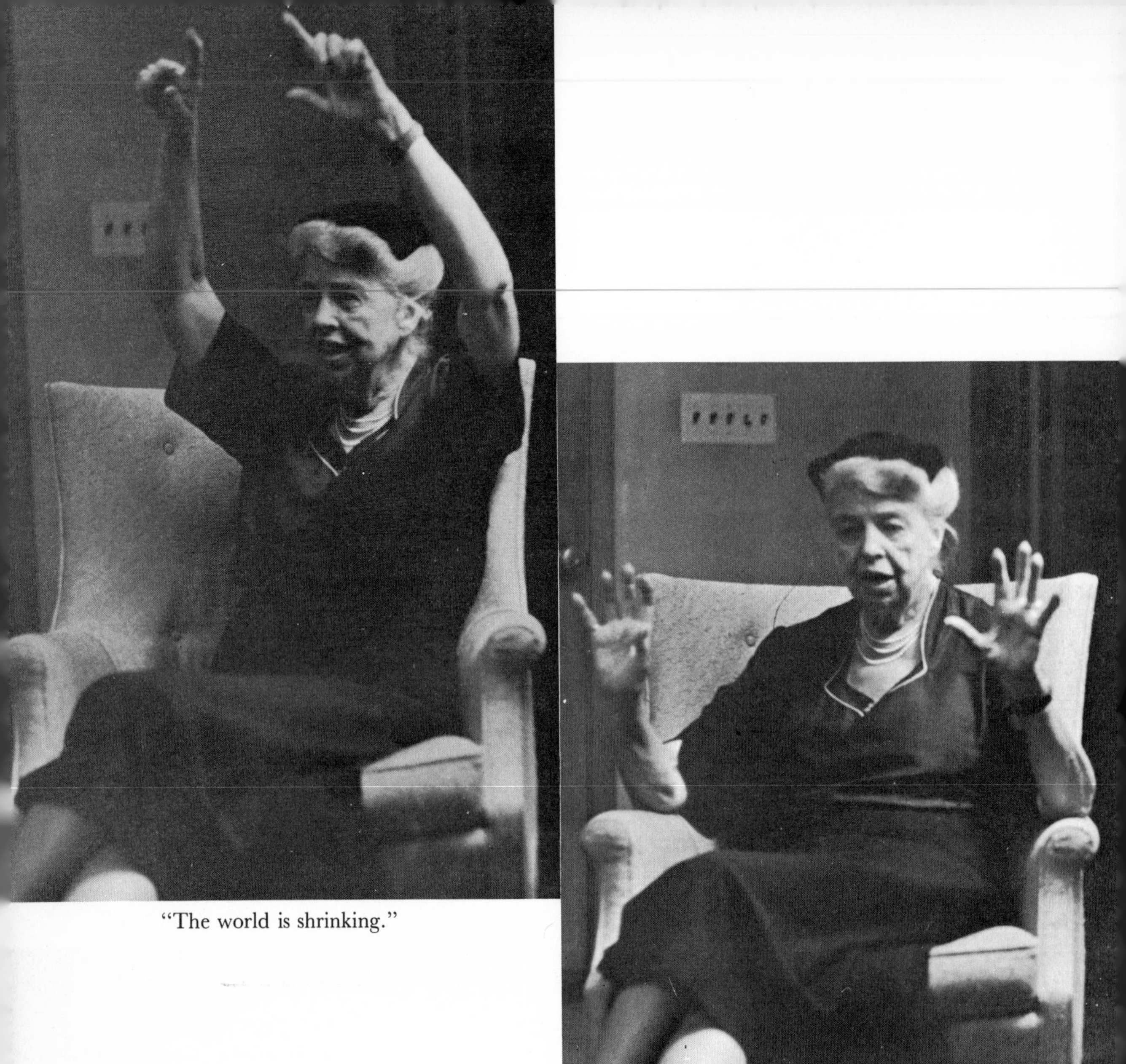

"The world is shrinking."

"The heart of America will soon fly to the heart of Asia in short hours."

"And yet, in Nikko, Japan, I overheard one American youngster in a temple, say, 'Gee, who was this Buddha . . . ?' "

"We need understanding, we need wisdom, we need patience."

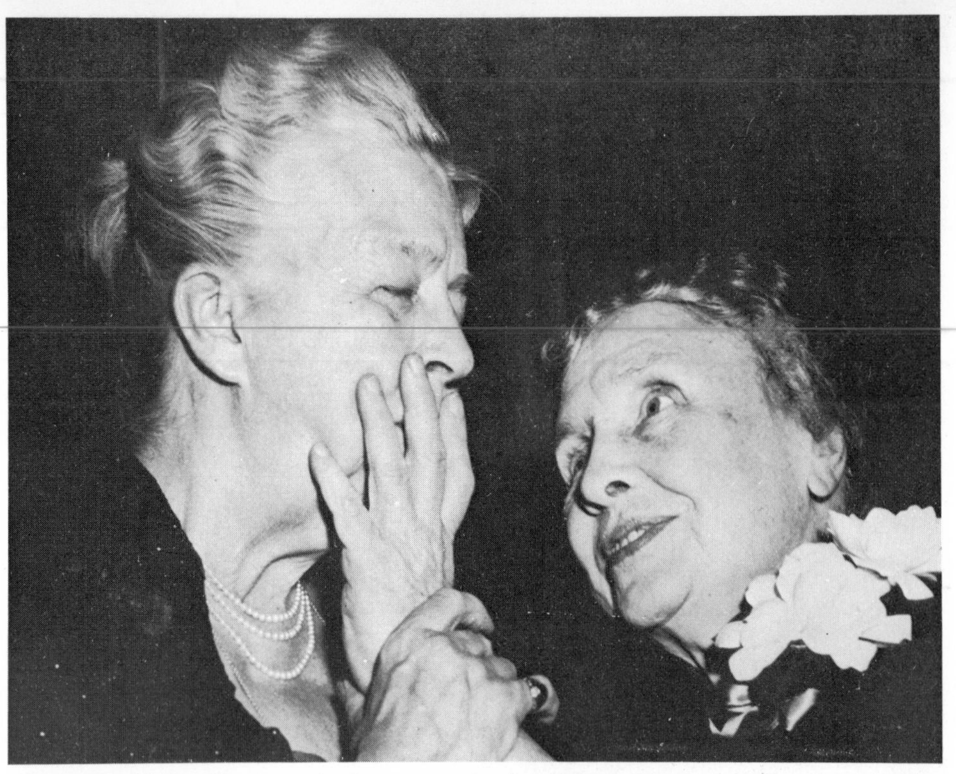

Talking with her lips to a deaf woman who hears better than most hearing people, a blind woman who sees better than most seeing people, and a speechless woman whose voice is heard around the world—Helen Keller.

Talking with her heart to the emotionally disturbed children of Wiltwyck School, a place she has long supported with time, money, picnics, energy, and most of all, love.

"And yet, in Nikko, Japan, I overheard one American youngster in a temple, say, 'Gee, who was this Buddha . . . ?' "

"We need understanding, we need wisdom, we need patience."

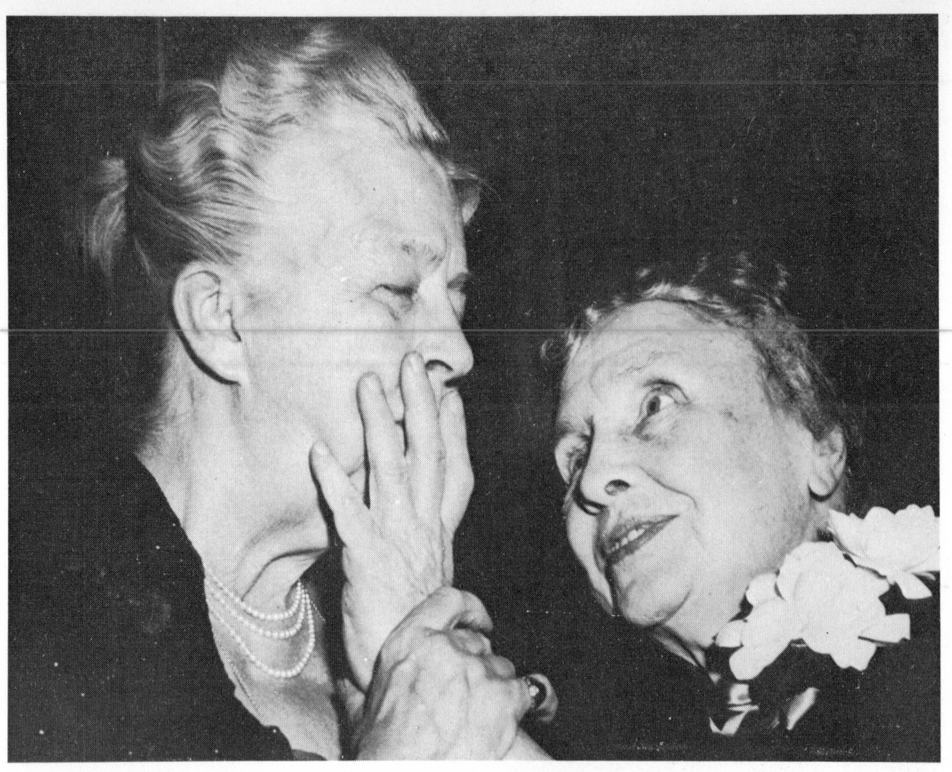

Talking with her lips to a deaf woman who hears better than most hearing people, a blind woman who sees better than most seeing people, and a speechless woman whose voice is heard around the world—Helen Keller.

Talking with her heart to the emotionally disturbed children of Wiltwyck School, a place she has long supported with time, money, picnics, energy, and most of all, love.

Never has she crossed a picket line, always has she fought against sweatshop labor, and hers was the strongest national voice pressuring for passage of the child labor amendment. She said again and again to any group who would listen, "You cannot be free if you cannot earn enough to eat and live decently." So she has earned the right to tell Walter Reuther or anybody else in labor that "I would like to see labor look upon problems not only as problems of organized labor but as problems of the country as a whole."

She told Adlai Stevenson to get in an old car and travel leisurely around the country finding out how people live and what they think. She told him that because she wanted him to win in 1952 and 1956. She pitted her political strength against Harry S. Truman and New York Governor Averell Harriman and supplied the pivotal force that helped swing the Democratic nomination to Stevenson. She campaigned for him on a stiff schedule of midnight trains, radio and TV, small towns, big cities, all kinds of parties, meetings, speeches that would have broken the backs of most other seventy-year-old great-grandmothers.

She could have been the Democratic nominee for the United States Senate from New York in 1946. President Truman said publicly that she would be highly acceptable as his vice-presidential running mate in 1948. Columnist Heywood Broun thought she would make a pretty good president, "because it seems to me that Eleanor Roosevelt has a deeper and closer understanding of the needs and aspirations of millions of Americans than any other person in public life." But always she said no. "The truth is I don't like politics especially," she said, "because I probably know too much about it—and the sacrifices it demands."

Star
The Evening Star

Harry S. Truman is listening attentively to Mrs. Roosevelt, as he always has. But both are individuals. When Truman came out for Averell Harriman for Democratic candidate for president at the 1956 convention, Eleanor Roosevelt delayed a trip abroad and held a press conference to tell why she was for Adlai Stevenson. Long before, President Truman had appointed her to the United Nations and was willing to have her run with him as vice-presidential candidate in 1948.

Whenever she stops traveling the world, the great and the humble of the world come to see her. The Churchills, Emperor Haile Selassie, Queen Juliana and Prince Bernhard of the Netherlands, Premier Nehru and Madame Pandit of India, the King and Queen of Greece. And here she is with Charles de Gaulle, Premier of France.

Talking to the Russian people was one thing . . .

. . . talking to Nikita Krushchev was another.

The only way she managed to keep the Secret Service men away from her during the White House days was her promise to learn how to use a gun and carry one in her car, which she did. This is a hand-made gun, a gift of the Afridi Tribesmen in the Khyber Pass. She didn't need it with Khrushchev because, as he himself said, "At least we didn't shoot each other. . . ." She still renews her pistol permit every year.

This is the Eleanor Roosevelt few ever see, the woman who lives in the stone cottage at Val Kill in Hyde Park, on a few acres of land deeded her by her husband, a woman who does her own shopping at roadside stands, reads poetry to her close friends, simply scrambles more eggs when unexpected guests come—as they always do. She is a woman who says warmly, "The greatest thing I have learned is how good it is to come home again."

Her children are scattered everywhere, and they always travel to see one another. She is shown here in blue jeans at the ranch home of her son Elliott and his wife Minnewa at Meeker, Colorado.

Christmas at Hyde Park, 1957. Wherever she goes, she buys presents to be brought back to her home, ticketed, docketed, and tucked away in a spacious cupboard for Christmastime for her five children, nineteen grandchildren, nine great grandchildren, and friends. With her in this picture are: grandchildren Haven (center) and Nina (right) and a friend, Mrs. Joseph P. Lash.

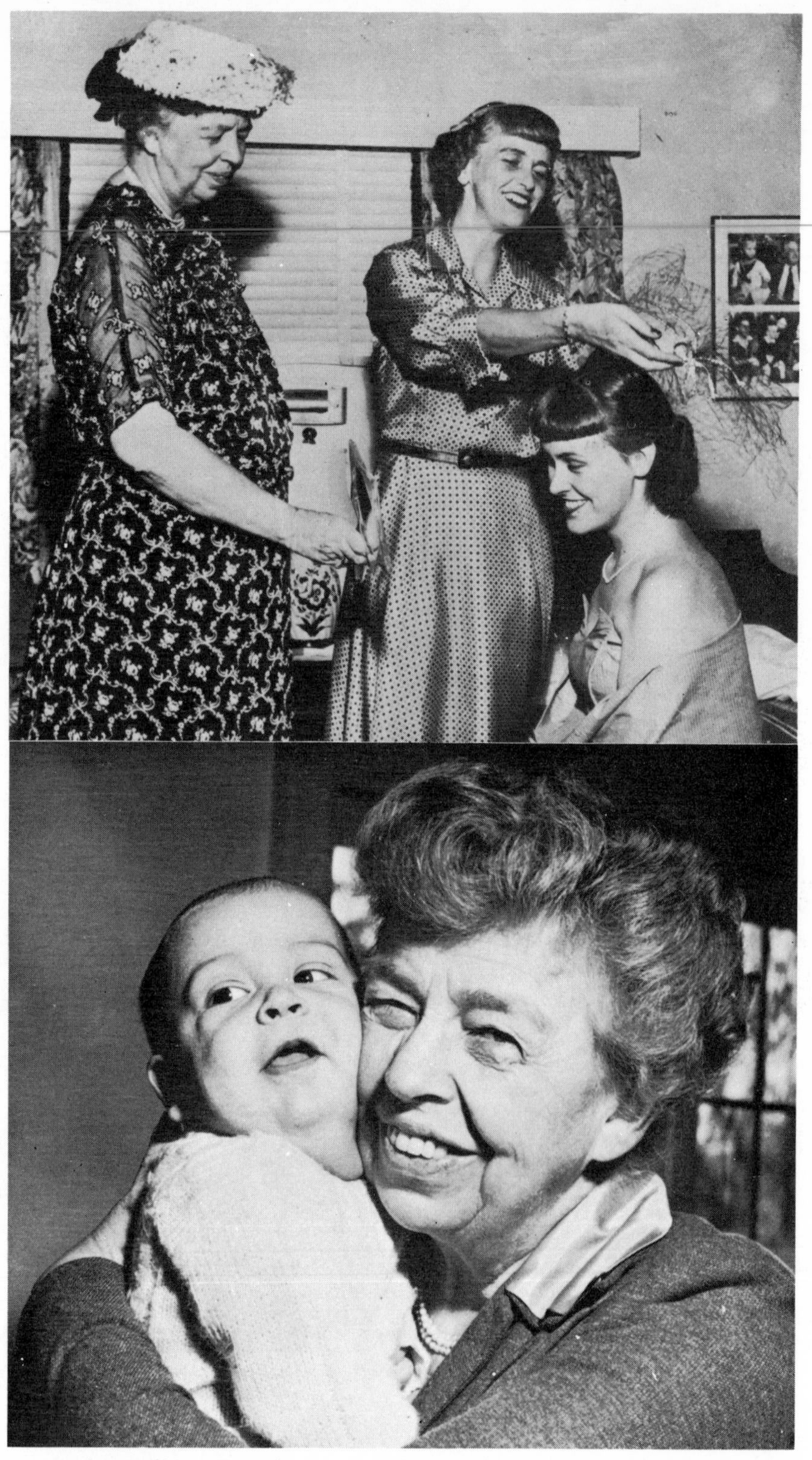

A granddaughter gets married, and a great-grandson is born.

"Of course the thing I am proudest of is that I have produced five children, all of whom are pretty nice people. I treasure the love of my children and the respect of my children, the most important part of my life. I promise that through those I love will be carried on what their father began."

Hyde Park, New York

Warm Springs, Georgia

Campobello

PAA
PAA
PAA PAA

"Of Course I Know—It's Mrs. Roosevelt"

10/11/1954, in celebration of Mrs. Roosevelt's 70th birthday

Drawn for Mrs. Roosevelt's seventieth birthday by Herblock for *Here and Now*, Simon and Schuster, Inc.